THE DYNAMICS OF INTERNATIONAL LAW

by

GEORG SCHWARZENBERGER

of Gray's Inn, Barrister-at-Law;
Director, London Institute of World Affairs;
Emeritus Professor of International Law
in the University of London

Published in 1976 by Professional Books Limited, Milton Trading Estate, Milton, near Abingdon, Oxon

ISBN 0 903486 18 0 (Paperback)
0 903486 19 9

This book has been typeset in Times by Inforum Limited of Portsmouth and printed in Great Britain by Professional Books Limited.

CONTENTS

To past futures
and future pasts

PREFACE

In a turbulent and, at least on the surface, rapidly changing world society, the problems connected with international law in motion deserve special attention.

In this field, the Doctrine of International Law has to make its own specific contribution. It is to find commensurate perspectives and techniques for coping with the major issues arising in a spirit of detachment from "deserving" causes, ideologies, institutions, and without fear or favour to any vested interest concerned.

The book is intended as a companion to *The Frontiers of International Law* (Stevens, London—1962) and *International Law and Order* (Stevens, London—1971). It is addressed to three categories of reader:

(1) The increasing number of postgraduate students who desire to balance specialised work in the various branches of international law by the study of more basic problems and receive guidance on such issues beyond the scope available in a textbook.

(2) Law teachers and students who wish to have some relevant essays more easily accessible than in the form in which they had first been published and to have them brought up to date, inter-related, pruned or expanded as the case requires.

(3) Legal practitioners, politicians, civil servants — national, international and supranational — and laymen who desire to make up their own minds on the relevance of international law in contemporary world society.

I am obliged to Messrs. Stevens & Sons, London, for permission to use in Chapters 3-7 material published in *Current Legal Problems* (1972 and 1973) and *The Year Book of World Affairs* (1972, 1974 and 1975), to Dr. A. Connelly, for reading the proofs and preparing the Tables of Cases and Treaties, and the Subect Index and to Mr. J. Stockdale for also reading the proofs and seeing the book through the press.

G.S.

LONDON
March 28, 1976

TABLE OF CASES

TABLE OF TREATIES

* Not yet in force.

Chapter 1

FUNDAMENTALS

"When we look at a thing, we must examine its essence."
Mao Tse-Tung, *A Single Spark Can Start a Prairie Fire* (1930)

This Chapter contains a description of the theme of the book, a restatement of the methods applied and a glossary of key words.

I—THE THEME

Chapter 2 on *Statics and Dynamics in International Law* is an attempt to find verifiable — or, with Karl Popper, falsifiable — criteria for evaluating asserted new rules of international law.

Chapter 3 on *Historical Models of International Law* aims at a comparative approach to the history of international law and presentation of the overabundant raw material, accumulated over more than three millenia, in five basic models.

Chapter 4 on *Equity in International Law* is intended as an assessment of the place of good faith, reasonableness and common sense in the dynamics of international law.

Chapter 5 on *The Law of Armed Conflict: A Civilised Interlude?* provides an analysis of the social factors conditioning the dynamics of the law of armed conflict.

Chapter 6 on *European Common Law* is concerned with the place of the Law of the European Communities in the context of the European legal heritage and the relation between various individual rules of international law and different levels of international and supranational integration.

Chapter 7 on *Civitas Maxima?* is intended to provide an empirical synopsis of the dynamics of law and order in contemporary world society.

II—METHODS

As with earlier writings, the essays in this book are based on inductive, inter-disciplinary and relativist approaches to international law.

On the *normative* level, the *inductive* approach to international law is an empirical technique, based on the authority of near-universal consent (as expressed in Article 38 of the Statute of the International Court of Justice), to safeguard international law against the subjectivism of deductive speculation and eclectic caprice, and the vested interests prone to use — and abuse — both. It has four distinctive features:

(1) Emphasis on the exclusive character of the three primary law-creating processes in international law: consensual understandings, international customary law, and the general principles of law recognised by civilised nations.

(2) Establishment of the "means for the determination of rules of law", as they are termed in Article 38 of the Statute of the International Court of Justice — the law-determining agencies and their elements — in accordance with rationally verifiable criteria.

(3) Awareness of the character of the rules of international law as the only binding norms of international law unless evidence is forthcoming that a principle, which has been abstracted from such rules, has itself acquired the character of an overriding rule.

(4) Realisation of the differences which exist between international law as applied in unorganised, partly organised and fully organised international societies.

On the level of *social* studies, the *inter-disciplinary* approach makes use of any facet of a phenomenon that, in relation to any particular problem, is of special significance.

This description is formal in that it merely underlines the relevance, for international law, of other disciplines concerned with international studies. If the emphasis is put on the substance of such investigations, this inter-disciplinary technique can also be described as *phenomenological.*

The *caveat* may be repeated that any inter-disciplinary statements and evaluations made in this book are to be understood as such and are not to be given any normative meaning.

Finally, in the field of *lex ferenda,* the *relativist* treatment of questions connected with the development of international law and organisation provides legitimate scope for imagination and creativeness, but imposes necessary controls of rational verification, indispensable in any field of serious study.

III—KEY WORDS

Community: social group which is more highly integrated than a society *(q.v.).*
Crime against Humanity: controversial extension of war crimes jurisdiction under the laws and customs of war. See also under *War Crimes.*
Crime against Peace: see above.
De facto revision: uncompleted process of *de jure* revision *(q.v.).*

De jure revision: process of revision completed in accordance with legal requirements.
Dynamics: motion, *e.g.,* law in motion. See also under *Statics.*
Hegemony: the position of factual pre-eminence in the relations between sovereign and equal States.
Ideology: idea or argument, employed to disguise in terms of abstract ideas or principles undisclosed interests, *e.g.,* alleged concern for human rights as an excuse for interfering with the internal affairs of another sovereign State.
Image: concept with a largely or predominantly visual element.
Inductive Approach: see above under II.
Inter-disciplinary Approach: see *ibid.*
Jus aequum: legal system in which rights are relative and must be exercised reasonably and in good faith.
Jus cogens: law binding irrespective of the will of individual parties.
Jus dispositivum: law capable of being modified by consensual engagements.
Jus strictum: legal system in which rights are absolute and may be exercised irrespective of equitable considerations.
Law: includes any norms *(q.v.)* intended to regulate social conduct which, if required, can be authoritatively determined on a basis of consent or compulsion and enforced by the application of external sanctions.
Law-creating Process: see above under I and II and below Chapter 2 (II).
Law-determining Agency: see *ibid.*
Law of Co-ordination: the law of a community *(q.v.)* which is characterised by freely accepted duties, rather than rights.
Law of Power: the law of a society *(q.v.)*, which is characterised by subservience to the interests of some, as distinct from those of the group as a whole.
Law of Reciprocity: the law of a social group which has features of a society and community *(q.v.)* and is characterised by a substantial equivalence of rights and duties.
Legal Order: legal system, embodying a *de facto* order *(q.v.)* and endowing it with the dignity of the law.
Legal Regime: system of legal rules which are reasonably coherent but are too specialised or subordinate to qualify as a legal order *(q.v.).*
Legitimation: recognition, confirmation, acceptance or justification of an existing or aspired to and, essentially, factual state of affairs.
Lex ferenda: law which it is desired to establish.
Lex imperfecta: law lacking external sanctions.
Lex lata: law in force.
Model: Intended to represent simply but accurately a particular facet of reality.
Norm: legal or moral rule, expressing an *Ought,* as distinct from an *Is.* See also under *Law.*

Order: state of affairs, characterised by the effective control of those subject to such a system by an essentially factual rather than normative (see under *Norm)* apparatus of force and power (see also under *Legal Order).*
Organised International Society: international society on the level of, *e.g.,* the confederate organisation of the United Nations and its Specialised Agencies.
Phenomenological Approach: the study of all or, at least, all significant manifestations of a problem (see above under II).
Power: the mean between influence and force. Power distinguishes itself from *influence* by reliance on external pressure as a background threat, and from *force* by preference for achieving its ends without the actual use of physical pressure.
Quasi-Order: an order which, like the League of Nations, is too weak or precarious to achieve its appointed task.
Relativist Approach: see above under II and below Chapter 2 (II).
Self-Defence: action required to forestall an imminent threat to a right or to redress the actual breach of such a right.
Self-Determination: formative principle of international relations, precariously incorporated in consensual international law.
Society: a loose type of association, as distinct from a community *(q.v.).*
Standard: optional norm *(e.g.,* the most-favoured-nation standard) which may be incorporated as a binding rule in a treaty and, in this case, qualifies the operation of an otherwise absolute principle, such as the principle of freedom of commerce.
Statics: state of rest, *e.g.,* of law at any particular moment. See also under *Dynamics.*
Utopia: proposal *de lege ferenda (q.v.),* incompatible with an existing political or social order (see also under *Ideology).*
War Crime: breach of the laws and customs of war, authorising the enemy State to exercise an extraordinary wartime jurisdiction against the person charged with the commission of a war crime. See also under *Crime against Humanity* and *Crime Against Peace.*

Chapter 2

STATICS AND DYNAMICS IN INTERNATIONAL LAW

"The possibility of the law changing is ever present: but that cannot relieve the Court from its obligation to render a judgment on the basis of the law as it exists at the time of its decision". Fisheries Jurisdiction Case (United Kingdom *v.* Iceland), International Court of Justice (1974)

Emphasis on the statics and dynamics of any branch of law varies according to the purposes of the inquiry. Thus, practitioners who attempt to assess their clients' chances in a lawsuit will tend to concentrate on the law likely to be applied in the case, bearing in mind the judicial, quasi-judicial or administrative character of the organ concerned and its personal composition. They will try to forecast official behaviour and, accordingly, adjust their presentation of the law in static or dynamic terms. In the *Nuclear Test Cases* (1974), the Prime Minister of Australia incurred the displeasure of the International Court of Justice by revealing publicly the potential accuracy of such forecasting techniques down to the last vote.[1]

Academic lawyers enjoy greater freedom in their approaches to the law. Admittedly, the amount of this freedom will vary according to the political environment and the degree of self-coordination individual lawyers consider opportune. Subject to such external factors, the treatment of a subject-matter will be primarily determined by the normative or interdisciplinary purpose of a particular study. In a systematic presentation, the law has to be frozen at a particular moment. If the purpose is that of an analysis of the law in a historical or social context, only the most pedestrian presentation will fail to convey the dynamics of the law.

Distorting emphasis on the statics or dynamics of the law may also be due to extrinsic causes. These may range from those behind the briefs of legal exponents of vested interests to those inspiring the emanations of committed scholarship. Products in these categories are not to be despised. They are likely to offer quotable evidence of the ideologies and utopias woven around the law. In the international field, a paper-gold medal should perhaps be awarded to the Sixth Committee of the General Assembly of the United Nations for unequalled excellence in the field of

[1] See, for instance, the Declaration on the subject by President Lachs and the Joint Declaration by five other members of the Court in the *Nuclear Tests Case (Australia v. France), I.C.J. Reports 1974,* p. 273, and, further, the writer's *International Law as Applied by International Courts and Tribunals,* Vol. III (1976), Chapters 15 (3) and 21.

legal ideology-mongering, with relevant *ad hoc* committees of the General Assembly as close runners-up.

I—THE STATICS OF INTERNATIONAL LAW

In any exploration of the statics and dynamics of international law, international lawyers could do worse than accept as self-denying ordinances duties which are imposed by Article 38 of the Court's Statute on the International Court of Justice.

In this context, it is important to appreciate a basic distinction discernible in Article 38. It is between law-creating processes (treaties, international customary law and general principles of law recognised by civilised nations) and law-determining agencies (subjects of international law, courts and writers) and, further, between the constituent elements of each of these law-determining agencies.[2]

II—RELATIVITY OF THE DISTINCTION BETWEEN THE STATICS AND DYNAMICS OF INTERNATIONAL LAW

Each of the law-creating processes enumerated in Article 38 of theStatute of the International Court of Justice provides scope for the dynamics of international law.

International Customary Law

Article 38 (1)(b) of the Statute of the International Court of Justice is probably the least adequately drafted section of the whole Article. What it is intended to convey is that the test of any rule asserted to form part of the body of international customary law is whether it corresponds to a general practice accepted as law, that is, whether it is regarded as legally binding.

For a rule of international customary law to come into existence, no particular form is required, nor must the rule have existed for any particular length of time. All that matters is that the generality of subjects of international law accepts the rule as law.

In view of the reciprocal character of the rules of international customary law, subjects of international law must necessarily accept the binding character of these rules as much against themselves as in their favour. It is one of the intrinsic features of the rules of international customary law that they are addressed to subjects of international law at large.

It also follows that the occasion on which a rule of international custom-

2 See, further, *ibid.*, Vol. I (1957), p. 25 *et seq.*

ary law happens to be formulated is immaterial. It may be in a conference protocol, the award of an international tribunal, the judgment of a national or international court, or it may be a product of legal Doctrine.

In the international customary law of *unorganised* international society, the dynamics work themselves out almost invisibly. They operate by way of a continuous process of give and take between the rules underlying the principle of Sovereignty and the other six fundamental principles of international customary law — Recognition, Consent, Good Faith, Freedom of the Seas, International Responsibility, and Self-Defence — and between those governing each of these latter principles.

Attempts to freeze these rules in unorganised and partly organised international society are likely to be made at various times by individual subjects of international law or any group of them, conferences, judicial organs and writers. Yet, insofar as other subjects of international law are concerned, any such effort by any element of a law-determining agency of international law is of merely persuasive authority.

Every subject of international law is entitled to its own view on the stage reached at any particular time in the interplay of the rules of international customary law. Complete anarchy might well be the result of such a complete freedom of self-evaluation. Actually, this risk is considerably mitigated by the working principle inherent in international customary law: the principle of reciprocity.

Treaty Law

The ever-swelling size of the leading treaty series offers abundant evidence of the frequent use made of the rules underlying the principle of consent. In this way, international customary law has always made it possible for the dynamics of international society to find expression in consensual superstructures, erected on the foundations of unorganised international society. Yet, unless third parties decide to co-operate, such consensual rules apply only between contracting parties.

As by any other multilateral treaty, members of international and supranational institutions may change, as they see fit, the interplay between the rules governing the seven fundamental principles of international customary law and supplement them by, or substitute for them, inter-related consensual principles. They are free to transfer to such institutions any powers, including quasi-legislative or legislative powers, for the adjustment of their future relations to changing needs. The only issues which arise in this context are questions of evidence: Has an asserted transfer of powers actually taken place and, if not, have members at least acquiesced in any particular arrogation of powers by institutional organs?

General Principles of Law

In the dynamics of international law, the significance of the general principles of law recognised by civilised nations varies according to the level of international or supranational integration on which they are invoked.

For instance, on the levels of unorganised and partly organised international society, the assertion of subjective responsibility as a general principle of law is likely to be countered by the invocation of the principle of objective responsibility as a counter-principle. Similarly, every legal maxim invoked as evidence of a general principle tends to be neutralised by a counter-maxim, and both are frequently of no higher authority than Chinese proverbs invented by Western wits.

On levels of higher integration as in the United Nations concerning staff relations, and in supranational communitites, greater opportunities exist for organs with decision-making powers to develop international law by reference to general principles of law or principles of law recognised by all the member States of the institution concerned. The judicial policies on the prohibition of the abuse of powers, evolved by the United Nations Administrative Tribunal, the ILO Administrative Tribunal and the Court of Justice of the European Communities, illustrate this proposition.[3]

It is tempting but hardly in accordance with the best standards of scholarship to use general principles of law developed on levels of higher international integration as evidence for the existence of equivalent principles or rules in existing international law on levels of lower integration or, altogether, to ignore these differences. To proceed in this manner is little more than special pleading — if for purposes of "advancing" international law.

III—LAW-MAKING IN THE UNITED NATIONS

In assessing the dynamics of international law in the United Nations system, including the Related Inter-Governmental Agencies, three assumptions made must be briefly stated:

(1) The United Nations constitutes the confederate framework of contemporary world society.

(2) The United Nations Charter and the constituent instruments of the Related Inter-Governmental Agencies represent consensual *jus cogens*.

In particular, the character of *jus cogens* attaches to the Principles embodied in Article 2 of the United Nations Charter. Yet, owing to the consensual character of this *jus cogens,* it extends to third parties only if they have estopped themselves from contesting their subjection to United Nations law.

[3] See, further, below, Chapter 4 under III (c), and *loc. cit.* above, note 1, Vol. III (1976), Chapter 41.

(3) According to the scheme of the Charter, none of the organs of the United Nations has legislative powers on substantive matters, as distinct from regulatory powers for internal purposes and emergency powers such as those of the Security Council under Chapter VII of the Charter. The powers entrusted to the General Assembly and auxiliary bodies such as the International Law Commission in the spheres of law-making are purely recommendatory.

Thus, until a convention "adopted" by the General Assembly of the United Nations is implemented by potential contracting parties, it remains a draft convention. Unless, as with international labour conventions, the constitution of a Related Agency attaches at least limited legal effects to the phase of adoption,[4] the jurisdiction of the plenary organs of these Agencies is similarly limited.

In particular, if organs fail to distinguish — as is the habit of the United Nations organs entrusted with prelegislative functions — between codification of existing law and its development, individual provisions of United Nations conventions cannot be lightly taken as evidence of their declaratory character. In each case, their character as *lex lata* or *lex ferenda* must be the subject of independent inquiry.

The Articles in the 1969 Vienna Treaties Convention on the voting rules for the adoption of a treaty at international conferences and the interpretation of treaties illustrate this proposition. The Convention is not even in force, and the drafting history of both groups of Articles would make it difficult to present either group as a straightforward codification of existing international law.[5]

Two Classes of U.N. Law?

In United Nations practice, a distinction is occasionally drawn between "hard" and "soft" law. In the former category are amendments of the Charter in accordance with Chapter XVIII and conventions initiated or adopted by the United Nations organs which become binding on States in accordance with the requirements of each of these conventions. In the latter are resolutions of the General Assembly on matters in which the General Assembly exercises a merely recommendatory jurisdiction and multilateral conventions, in force or not in force, which purport to be declaratory of international law.

The flaw in the distinction between "hard" and "soft" law is that it takes for granted what has yet to be proved. It is that "soft law" is law at all. The test is whether, under Article 38 of the Statute of the International Court of Justice, an alleged rule corresponds to the requirements of primary or

[4] Article 19 (5). ILO Constitution.
See also A. J. P. Tammes, *Decisions of International Organs as a Source of International Law*, Hague Academy of International Law, Vol. 94 (1959), p. 265 *et seq.*

[5] See, further, L.B. Sohn, *Voting in U.N. Conferences*, 69 A.J.I.L. (1975), p. 318 *et seq.*, and the writer's *International Law and Order* (1971), p. 110 *et seq.*

secondary law-creating processes, the latter being illustrated by regulations of international institutions. If this is the case, it is a legal rule. If not, it cannot obtain this character as a reincarnation of the notion of *lex imperfecta*. Whatever significance *lex imperfecta* may have in international morality, including the writings of the naturalist school of international law Doctrine and international ideology-mongering, it is not international law.

The distinction between "hard" and "soft" United Nations law recalls an experience of the League of Nations era: the Interpretative Resolution relating to Article 16 of the Covenant, adopted in 1921 by the League Assembly. It failed to comply with the conditions laid down for a revision of the Covenant but undermined the credibility of its sanctions provisions and set in motion the eroding process of a *de facto* revision of the League Covenant.[6]

Compliance with International Law Standards

The United Nations Charter, like the League Covenant before it, makes its revision a complicated and protracted affair. Yet, whenever the necessary consensus exists, the feat can, and has been, accomplished.

Similarly, the League of Nations and United Nations have initiated a considerable number of multilateral conventions. The choice of topics as well as the number and identity of contracting parties are reliable indicators of such consensus as exists at any time on the direction of the dynamics of international law.

If such consensus blossoms most freely in the fields of diplomatic privileges, communications and humanitarianism, rather than in politically sensitive spheres, this is not accidental. It may be symptomatic of the stability of the political *de facto* order underlying international law and/or may indicate the unwillingness of the leading Powers to enter into legally binding commitments on central issues of world power politics.

Even in areas of apparent agreement and "hard" law, actual consensus may be narrowed by allowing contracting parties to qualify their acceptance of conventions by declarations, reservations and objections to such declarations and reservations.

If consensus was to be attained in decisive areas such as nuclear devices or activitites in outer space, novel clauses had to make their appearance. In a more circuitous form than more traditional renunciation and reservation clauses, they serve the same end: in case of need, prompt release from burdensome treaty obligations entered into and a switch-over from international law to unrestrained freedom of action.

Similarly, on matters such as the protection of foreign investments, on which governments of capital-importing countries are exposed to severe

[6] For the text of the Interpretative Resolution, adopted October 4, 1921, see A. B. Keith, *Speeches and Documents on International Affairs 1918-1937* (1938), p. 68 *et seq.*, and, further, the writer's *Power Politics* (1964), p. 277 *et seq.*

internal pressures, the price of agreement between capital-exporting and capital-importing countries may be prohibitive. If capital-exporting countries persist, they may have to be content with inadequate protective clauses of a substantive character and provisions for the settlement of investment disputes which amount to little more than *pacta de contrahendo.*[7]

Lowering the Sights?

Claims by contemporary institutions to attach to their pronouncements a law-making character against third parties are in the best tradition of the Concert of Europe.

It is understandable that the slow and cumbersome nature of traditional treaty-making should invite a search for more effective alternatives. Setbacks such as the Law of the Sea and Humanitarian Law in Armed Conflict Conferences of 1974 and 1975 or the 1975 Conference on Review of the Nuclear Non-Proliferation Treaty let feasible short-cuts appear even more desirable to would-be international legislators.

If subjects of international law desire closer international integration in the field of international law-making or any other joint activity, this can be attained. Functional and territorial sub-models of the unionist model offer such opportunities.[8] Yet if those concerned desire to maintain simultaneously an almost untrammelled freedom of action, the result is not "soft" law but pseudo-law: a "law" that has all the attractions of eating one's cake and keeping it.

The purely recommendatory jurisdiction in the field of law-making of the United Nations General Assembly and the plenary organs of most of the Related Agencies makes it difficult to accept the assimilation of resolutions adopted by such organs, however often reiterated, to practices of the member States accepted as law. Thus, speaker after speaker in the 1948 General Assembly extolled the Universal Declaration of Human Rights but emphasised its purely moral and standard-setting character.

Conversely, in the 1946 General Assembly, delegates of member States not only voted for the acceptance of the Nuremberg Principles as an integral part of existing international law but also committed their governments in supporting speeches to this interpretation of the London Charter of the Nuremberg International Military Tribunal (1945) and its findings. In doing so, they may well have created estoppels against their countries denying in future the character of these principles as part of *lex lata.*[9]

In cases in which member States are not estopped from raising the

7 See, for instance, the 1965 Convention on the Settlement of Investment Disputes between States and Nationals of other States (Cmnd. 2745 — 1965) and, further, the writer's *Foreign Investments and International Law* (1969), p. 135 *et seq.*

8 See below, Chapter 3 under II (5) (c).

9 See, further, *loc. cit.* above, note 1, Vol. II (1968), p. 526 *et seq.*

purely recommendatory character of resolutions adopted by plenary organs or their merely standard-setting character, doubts on the binding character of such resolutions arise in at least seven other typical situations.

(1) if a subject-matter is not covered by treaty because of a manifest lack of consensus;

(2) if the subject-matter is covered by treaties which third parties consider to constitute departures from international customary law;

(3) if the subject-matter is covered by treaties not yet in force;

(4) if the resolution is to be implemented by a treaty;

(5) if reservations made by more than a negligible number of members during the deliberation of the subject-matter in the plenum and committees of the recommendatory organ concerned are so far-reaching as to create serious uncertainty on the scope of the alleged rule;

(6) if rules formulated are openly directed against particular States or are so narrowly formulated as to amount to *ad hoc* law;

(7) if the voting rules of the recommendatory organ on important issues are ignored and replaced by more summary forms of ascertaining consensus.

Depending on circumstances, even resolutions in any of these seven categories may have a limited relevance. As with repetitive resolutions challenging the standards of international customary law regarding the protection of foreign property abroad, they may initiate or complete a process of desuetude and assist in removing a particular rule from the sphere of International Responsibility to that of Sovereignty.

The Operators' Retort

Institutional operators may consider that, in a universalist system, the difference between a practice accepted as law and a practice accepted by the United Nations or other universalist institutions is, at the most, one of degree and, for all practical purposes, can be ignored with impunity by steam-roller majorities. In its time, each of the two hegemonial world Powers has used and abused the compact majority at its disposal in the United Nations.

Even in these cases, the *jus cogens* embodied in the Principles of the United Nations constitutes a limitation of the arrogation of powers by a General Assembly run wild.[10] Yet, it must be admitted that, in two contingencies, disregard of the Organisation's *jus cogens* by a majority becomes unverifiable. The first is that of the organ concerned refusing to request an advisory opinion from the judicial guardian of the Organisation. The second is that of the Court itself weakening in its guardianship of the law by allowing itself to become a "co-operative" Court which takes

10 See, further, *loc. cit.* above, note 1, Vol. III (1976), Chapters 14, 21 and 25.

its cues from the Sixth Committee of the General Assembly or other extraneous quarters, rather than Article 38 of its Statute.

In the following two Sections, the hypotheses advanced in this Section will be more closely tested in relation to two key Resolutions, adopted in 1974 by the General Assembly: those on Defining Aggression and on the Economic Rights and Duties of States.

IV – DEFINING AGGRESSION

General Assembly Resolution 3314 (XXIX)

Having adopted Resolution 3314 (XXIX) on December 14, 1974, the United Nations General Assembly congratulated itself on having brought the task of defining aggression to a successful conclusion.

Considering over half a century's history of disagreement on the subject since the early days of the League of Nations, this claim calls for closer examination.[11]

Contents and Status

Primary Definition. In Article 1 of the Resolution, aggression is defined as "the use of armed force by a State against the sovereignty, territorial integrity or political independence of another State, or in any other manner inconsistent with the Charter of the United Nations, as set out in this definition."

According to the Explanatory Note to Article 1 embodied in the Resolution, the term *State* is employed without prejudice to questions of recognition or membership of the United Nations.

"Without prejudice to questions of recognition" must mean that the freedom of a subject of international law not to recognise an entity as one possessing the qualities enumerated in Article 1 remains unimpaired by the Resolution. Thus, as in unorganised international society, every subject of international law remains free to decide for itself whether an entity which it has not recognised is entitled to be covered by the Resolution.

If the explanatory note is taken seriously, as it must be, the Resolution fails to provide guidance in relation to action against non-recognised governments in Vietnam- and Korea-types of situation.

Presumption of Aggression. In Article 2 of the Resolution, a presumption is created to the effect that "the first use of armed force by the State in contravention of the Charter" constitutes *prima facie* evidence of an act of aggression unless the Security Council decides otherwise.

11 In the words of Mr. Rossides (Cyprus) in the Sixth Committee of the U.N. Gen. Ass. (1471st meeting, October 8, 1974 — A/C.6/SR 1471, p. 5), "since work on defining aggression has begun in the League of Nations, its completion has been held up by one impediment or another for fifty years".

See, further, J. Stone, *Aggression and World Order* (1958), p. 27 *et seq.*, and *loc. cit.* above, note 6 (1964), p. 276 *et seq.*

Reserving for subsequent treatment the compatibility of the presumption created by Article 2 with the United Nations Charter, it may be wondered how the first use of armed force is to be determined in cases of border wars in remote areas with ill-defined frontiers such as those between India and China, India and Pakistan, and Mali and Upper Volta.

Auxiliary Definitions. In Article 3 of the Resolution, a whole series of further acts are classified as acts of aggression but the list is not intended to be exclusive. They range from temporary occupation and bombardment of the territory of another State to "the use of armed forces of one State, which are within the territory of another State with the agreement of the receiving State, in contravention of the conditions provided for in the agreement of any extension of their presence in such territory beyond the termination of the agreement".

It may be assumed that hegemonial interventions such as those of the Soviet Union in Berlin (1953), Hungary (1956) and Czechoslovakia (1968) fall under the last head.[12]

Further intriguing questions are raised by another set of circumstances: "The sending by or on behalf of a State of armed bands, groups, irregulars or mercenaries, which carry out acts of armed force against another State of such gravity as to amount to the acts listed above, or its substantial involvement therein".[13]

Reservation. The contingencies amounting to aggression under Articles 1-3 of the Resolution are subject to a major reservation in Article 7: "Nothing in this definition, and in particular Article Three, could in any way prejudice the right of self-determination, freedom and independence, as derived from the Charter, of peoples forcibly deprived of that right and referred to in the Declaration on principles of international law concerning friendly relations and co-operation among States in accordance with the Charter of the United Nations, particularly peoples under colonial and racist regimes or other forms of alien domination, nor the right of these peoples to struggle to that end and to seek and receive support, in accordance with the principles of the Charter and in conformity with the above mentioned Declaration".

The reservation creates far-reaching exceptions to the cases of aggression enumerated in Articles 1-3 of the Resolution. Moreover, in Article 7, at least three controversial assertions are made:

(1) It is considered possible to "derive" from the United Nations Charter a right of self-determination, freedom and independence of peoples forcibly deprived of this right and referred to in Resolution 2625 (XXV), adopted earlier by the General Assembly: the Declaration on Principles of International Law concerning Friendly Rela-

12 See, however, L.I. Bretžnev, as quoted by G.I. Tunkin, *Voelkerrechtstheorie* (1972), p. 482.
13 Article 3 (g).

tions and Co-operation among States in accordance with the Charter of the United Nations. In particular, "peoples under colonial and racist regimes or other forms of alien domination" are to be regarded as peoples forcibly deprived of the right of self-determination, freedom and independence.

(2) These deprived peoples are considered to have a right to "struggle" towards self-determination, freedom and independence, as derived from the United Nations Charter.

(3) These deprived peoples are endowed with the further right to "seek and receive support", but only "in accordance with the principles of the Charter" and "in conformity with the above mentioned Declaration", that is, the Declaration embodied in General Assembly Resolution 2625 (XXV).

The United Nations Charter does not provide any rights for peoples under the territorial control of member States, and even less so of non-member States, other than on a consensual basis in trust territories and former League Mandates.

Resolution 2625 (XXV) — apart from being adopted without vote on the occasion of 25th Anniversary Celebrations of the entry into force of the United Nations Charter, and its interpretation being subject to the views expressed, positions taken and reservations made by individual members in the plenum, committees and written communications — does not carry matters any further. Like the subsequent Resolution on the Definition of Aggression, it does not purport to enlarge or diminish the scope of the United Nations Charter, including its provisions concerning cases in which the use of force is lawful.[14]

Thus, it would be supererogatory to speculate on the additional rights under United Nations law or practice, granted by either Resolution to peoples in the position of Eritreans in Ethiopia, Kurds in Iraq, Nagas in India or New Guineans (West Iranians) and South Moluccans in Indonesia.

Status. Resolution 3314 (XXIX) was adopted by the Sixth Committee of the General Assembly and recommended to the General Assembly without vote. Similarly, it was adopted without vote by the General Assembly but, like Resolution 2625 (XXV), subject to all the views expressed, positions taken and reservations made by individual members in the committee and plenary stages of the Resolution in the General Assembly.

It may be questioned whether the General Assembly's practice of adopting resolutions by consensus is compatible with the provisions of Article

[14] U.N.Y.B. 1970, p. 792.
See, further, *loc. cit.* above, note 1, Vol. II (1968), p. 50 *et seq.*, and Vol. III (1976), Chapter 19 (4).

18 of the United Nations Charter. All decisions, including recommendations, of the General Assembly require an actual vote, and decisions on important questions require a two-thirds majority of the members present and voting. Voting is a formal expression of will or opinion in favour of or against a proposition or abstention from taking either course. Adoption of a resolution by consensus is the substitution of a different procedure: it is daring minorities to dissent. Their right to an automatic vote is replaced by a procedure which requires a potentially unpopular initiative. It means introducing into the democratic processes of a plenary organ a form of majority rule which may be deterrent in its discouragement of dissent.

Normative Critique

Resolution 3314 (XXIX) provides some clues to its legal relevance:

(1) *Absolute Prohibition of Aggression?*
"No consideration of whatever nature, whether political, economic, military or otherwise, may serve as a justification for aggression".

Read by itself, Article 5 (1) appears to suggest that, if an act is classified as aggressive in accordance with Articles 1-3 of the Resolution, any pragmatic considerations have to be ignored as possible grounds of justification. Yet, a relativist element is introduced by the freedom of evaluation conceded to the Security Council in Articles 2 and 3 (1) of the Resolution to take into consideration "other relevant circumstances, including the fact that the acts concerned or their consequences are not of sufficient gravity".

The Resolution remains silent on the contingency of the Security Council failing to reach the requisite majority decision under Article 27 (3) of the United Nations Charter or being prevented from making a substantive decision because of the exercise of the veto power by one of its permanent members. In this contingency, the situation remains as it was when, in the era of United States hegemony in the United Nations, the General Assembly attempted to circumnavigate a deadlock in the Security Council by its Uniting for Peace Resolution (377 (V)). Every member State remains free to make its own evaluation.

(2) *Crime against Peace?*
"A war of aggression is a crime against international peace. Aggression gives rise to international responsibility".

The first doubt which arises is whether every act of aggression in the meaning of the Resolution amounts to a war of aggression or only those aggressive acts which create a state of war in the traditional sense but "regardless of a declaration of war", or, in themselves or their consequences, are of especial gravity.

Subject to further attention to be given to the second sentence of Article 5 (2) of the Resolution, both views are tenable. Whichever is preferred, a war of aggression, once established, is classified as a war crime in the wider sense of the Nuremberg and Tokyo Principles: as a crime against international peace.[15] Thus, in the absence of any international organ of criminal adjudication, every member State is entitled under the Resolution to exercise an extraordinary criminal jurisdiction over persons alleged to have been responsible for a war of aggression and may pass sentences, from the death penalty downwards, on alleged criminals against peace in its power. If this right were exercised on the basis of, in all likelihood, conflicting evaluations by individual member States, the chaotic effects of any implementation of the Resolution beggar imagination.

The second sentence of Article 5 (2) of the Resolution on aggression giving rise to international responsibility follows the sentence on the classification of a *war* of aggression as a crime against international peace. The juxtaposition may be intended as a contrast between acts of aggression amounting to a war of aggression and others falling short of a war of aggression and, therefore, involving merely tortious responsibility to make reparation for an illegal act. Yet, the sentence can also be read as applying to both types of aggressive acts and, in both cases, involving tortious responsibility, in the former case additional to the criminal responsibility, which is asserted in the first sentence of Article 5 (2).

(3) *Non-Recognition:*
"No territorial acquisition or special advantage resulting from aggression are (*sic*) or shall be recognised as lawful".

The duty of not recognising the fruits of illegal action is a minimal, if sometimes merely implied, obligation which is incumbent upon members of any collective system. It was implied in Article 10 of the Covenant of the League of Nations, and is implied in Article 2 (4) of the United Nations Charter. Article 5 (3) of Resolution 3314 articulately spells out this duty.

(4) *Supremacy of the U.N. Charter*
Article 6 is the key Article of the Resolution:

"Nothing in this definition shall be construed as in any way enlarging or diminishing the scope of the Charter, including its provisions concerning cases in which the use of force is lawful".

Under the Charter, primary responsibility for the maintenance of international peace and security rests with the Security Council and, under Chapter Seven of the Charter, the Security Council has far-reaching discretionary powers in this field.

In this respect, Resolution 3314 suffers from a serious flaw. It purports to establish rebuttable presumptions of acts which are incompatible with the duties of States under the United Nations Charter. In attempting to determine what are *prima facie* aggressive acts, the General Assembly presumes to curtail the sphere of discretion granted under the Charter to the

15 See, further, *loc. cit.* above, note 1 Vol. II (1968), p. 478 *et seq.*

Security Council and forces on the Security Council the alternative between concurring with this determination in any particular case or expressing its dissent.

Such presumptions reverse the position under international customary law and the United Nations Charter. In accordance with the presumption in favour of the good faith of any subject of international law in general and any party to a treaty, the good faith of every subject of international law must be presumed. Thus, any action taken by a member State is presumed to be legal until and unless the Security Council has determined that it constitutes a threat to or a breach of international peace and security.

The difference between the positions under the Charter and the Resolution becomes evident in the case of the exercise of the veto power by one of the permanent members of the Security Council. In this contingency, under the Charter the presumption in favour of the good faith of the State arraigned remains operative. Under the Resolution, the opposite would be true: The *prima facie* classification of an act as aggressive would stand.

Similarly, in such a situation, under the Charter and Article 6 of the Resolution, the State which had taken the action impugned would be entitled to claim that it had acted in the exercise of the right of self-defence or collective defence against armed attack under Article 51 of the Charter. In accordance with the arithmetic of the "first" use of armed force under Article 2 of the Resolution, the position might well be reversed.

The changes in emphasis in the Resolution from the Charter and the Security Council to an apparent automatism in determining aggression are brain children of a mentality similar to that which has led to a departure from the Charter in the change in emphasis from voting in accordance with Article 18 of the Charter to the adoption of General Assembly resolutions by consensus.

United Nations operators may consider such changes to fall short of a breach of the Charter. If voting by consensus is not to become a practice in which dissenting members acquiesce, they can no longer afford to remain silent. They will have to challenge any proposal for "voting" by consensus in each individual case or, at least, state once and for all for the record that they will treat any "vote" by consensus as a non-vote.

In relation to the presumptions established by Resolution 3314, an additional remedy is at hand. These presumptions run counter to the measuring rod of Article 6 of the Resolution itself. If, as is submitted, these presumptions are contrary to the Charter, such a finding strengthens the case for emphasising what, in any case, is correct: the purely recommendatory character of the Resolution. If for no other reason, it must be ignored because of its unconstitutional character.

Inter-Disciplinary Critique

The shortcomings of the General Assembly's definition of aggression are inherent in the task of squaring this particular circle.

Aggression as an Ideology

In a system of open power politics as it existed, for instance, in pre-1914 international society, the distinction between legal and illegal war is unlikely to occur under international customary law. Unless limitations such as the requirement of at least a formal declaration of war are incorporated in treaties, any evaluation of acts as aggressive or defensive is of a purely moral character.

In systems of power politics in disguise such as the League of Nations, the Kellogg Pact and the United Nations, a distinction between legal and illegal resort to war or force is made. Yet, whether any particular resort to war or force is legal or illegal remains largely a matter of self-evaluation by every party concerned or, as in the United Nations, by at least each veto-Power.

In community systems of law, resort to force is severely limited and its exercise closely controlled by judicial organs. Even the right of self-defence may be exercised only within the narrowest confines. On this level, all forcible acts other than those which are clearly lawful can credibly be treated as illegal, and the breach of these rules can be visited with civil and criminal penalties.

If, in a system of community law, the need arose to define aggression, it could be most conveniently defined by reference to, for instance, self-defence. Thus, any action which was not covered by self-defence or other lawful forms of the use of force would be illegal.

It would be equally possible, and hardly require half a century's efforts, to define aggression in international law in a similar way, that is, by reference to self-defence and collective defence, and treat any other threat or use of force as illegal.

Yet, little would be gained unless three further steps were taken: organs with judicial or quasi-judicial powers would have to be authorised to adjudicate automatically on the lawfulness of, for instance, any particular action under Articles 2 (4), 51, 106 and 107 of the United Nations Charter; these organs would require powers to grant interim injunctions, and they would have to be able to enforce compliance with their orders.

In other words, what is implied in any quest for a commensurate definition of aggression — or, preferably, self-defence and collective defence — is the postulate of an effective and overriding legal order. In any system of power politics, open or in disguise, this would be a contradiction in terms.

Functions of the Ideology

Definitions such as those contained in General Assembly Resolution 3314 have their uses. They do not create any legal commitments. On challenge, they can be played down as mere guidelines and working tools. While they do not commit anybody to anything, everybody is free to use them for purposes of castigating his opponents as aggressors and criminals against peace.

Moreover, reservations such as those contained in Article 7 of Resolution 3314 offer splendid opportunities to reassert claims to "rights" which if they are not rights under international law can be presented as if they were at least international law in the making. Thus, what in systems of world power politics must remain a utopia can instantly be employed as a handy political ideology.

V — TOWARDS AN ECONOMIC WORLD ORDER?

General Assembly Resolution 3281 (XXIX)

Resolution 3281 (XXIX), embodying a Charter of Economic Rights and Duties of States and adopted by the United Nations General Assembly on December 12, 1974, has a fascinating background story.

It probably owes its origin to a casual table talk between two senior Netherlands delegates during one of the Sessions of the General Assembly in the mid-sixties. At the 1972 UNCTAD Conference in Santiago de Chile, the President of Mexico resuscitated the idea in a surprise intervention. From then onwards, it gathered momentum until, on the recommendation of the Second Committee, it came before the plenum of the General Assembly in 1974.[16]

Contents and Status

According to the Preamble, a fundamental purpose of the Charter of Economic Rights and Duties is to promote the establishment of a "new international economic order, based on equity, sovereign equality, interdependence, common interest and co-operation among all States, irrespective of their economic and social systems".

More concretely, the General Assembly expressed its desire to contribute to the creation of conditions for the attainment of wide prosperity among all countries and of higher standards of living for all peoples, the acceleration of the economic growth of developing countries, and the protection, preservation and enhancement of the environment.

16 For some of the material for a fascinating background story, see Netherlands Minister Bot's Speeches in the Second Committee of the U.N. General Assembly (October 22, 1965 and October 18, 1966), suggesting a "Charter of Development"; the Address given by President Luis Echeverria Alvarez of Mexico at the 92nd Plenary Meeting of the Third UNCTAD Conference (April 19, 1972); the Economic Declaration, adopted at the 5th Meeting of Non-Aligned Countries, Algiers, September 13, 1973, and the Declaration and Programme of Action on the Establishment of a New International Economic Order (U.N. Gen. Ass. Resolutions 3201 and 3202 (S — VI), May 1 1974 — both adopted without vote).

See also E.O. Rabasa, Proc. A.S.I.L. 1974, p. 302 *et seq.*, and F. Parkinson, *Latin American Foreign Policies in the Era of Detente,* 50 *International Affairs* (1974), pp. 443-444.

Principles. In a similarly wide sweep, fifteen fundamental principles, enumerated in a non-exhaustive list, range from sovereignty, non-intervention and abstention from attempts at seeking hegemonial positions or spheres of influence *via* sovereign equality to free access to and from the sea by land-locked countries "within the frame-work" of the other fourteen principles, and the fulfilment in good faith of international obligations.

Rights and Duties. The economic rights of States, set out in twenty-eight Articles, include permanent sovereignty over a State's wealth, natural resources and economic activities; the right to nationalise, expropriate or transfer ownership of foreign property against appropriate compensation; co-operation in the exploitation of natural resources "shared by two or more countries"; the right to associate in organisations of primary commodity producers, and the right of every State to benefit from the advances and developments in science and technology for the acceleration of its economic and social development.

In the catalogue of economic duties, the emphasis is on taking especially into account the interests of "developing" countries, on promoting the achievement of "general and complete disarmament under effective international control" and on utilising the resources freed for purposes of economic and social development, "allocating a substantial portion of such resources as additional means for the development needs of developing countries".

The elimination of "colonialism, apartheid, racial discrimination, neocolonialism and all forms of foreign aggression, occupation and domination" is considered to constitute a prerequisite of economic and social development and formulated as an individual and collective right *and* duty of all States.

Status. Resolution 3281 is intended as a recommendation and the basis for more detailed consideration by the General Assembly of the economic rights and duties of States.

The Resolution was adopted by one hundred and twenty votes against six, with ten abstentions. The six countries voting against the Resolution were Belgium, Denmark, Germany, Luxembourg, the United Kingdom and the United States of America. Those abstaining were Austria, Canada, France, Ireland, Israel, Italy, Japan, the Netherlands, Norway and Spain. Some countries as, for instance, India abstained from voting on individual clauses of the Charter but voted in favour of the Resolution as a whole.

The Charter is probably best viewed as a tentative framework for further discussions and the elaboration of more concrete guidelines on the substantive issues of an international economic order. As a recommendation, the Charter is well within the General Assembly's jurisdiction under Articles 10 and 13 of the United Nations Charter.

The remarkable degree of consensus attained is impressive. Whether, as happened with the Universal Declaration of Human Rights, the Charter will be subject to a severe process of contraction if and when its recommendations are to be translated into actual legal obligations, remains to be seen.

It should also be noted that none of the nine members of the European Communities voted in favour of the Resolution. They split, however, on the question of whether to abstain or vote against the Resolution. In this respect, the Benelux countries were similarly divided.

Critique

The Charter of Economic Rights and Duties of States attacks the unresolved problem of an international economic order in a more commensurate framework than Chapter IX of the United Nations Charter and the constituent instruments of its Related Agencies for economic and social co-operation in the United Nations system.[17]

Thus, this blueprint deserves both immanent and transcendental criticism, the former based on the assumptions made in the Resolution, and the latter based on assumptions which possibly differ from those made in the Resolution.

Immanent Criticism. On the assumptions made in the Charter, nine points may be selected for critique:

(1) *Terminology.* The terms *colonialism* and *neo-colonialism,* employed in Article 16 of the Resolution should be clarified so as to include overland expansion — what, in the words of Chinese and Albanian delegates, is termed social imperialism — and oppression practised by any country against ethnically different groups.[18]

(2) *Economic Responsibility.* The duty of making restitution and providing full compensation for countries affected by coercive policies under Article 16 of the Resolution is described in the same Article as an economic responsibility. It would be advisable to clarify whether this unusual term is intended as a contrast to legal responsibility. In this eventuality the whole provision would best be deleted or relegated to a Chapter of its own, possibly entitled: For gullibles only.

(3) *Permanent Sovereignty.* This term is as meaningless in the Charter of Economic Rights and Duties of States as in the repetitive resolutions passed on this topic over the years by the General Assembly.

At least potentially, any exercise of sovereignty must be conceived

[17] See, further, the Report on *A New United Nations Structure for Global Co-operation* by the Group of Experts on the Structure of the United Nations System (U.N. Doc. E/AC. 62/9 — May 28, 1975) and the writer's *Economic World Order?* (1970), p. 17 *et. seq.*

[18] See, further, *loc. cit.* above, note 7 (1969), pp. 16-17.

as limitable. If it could not be limited by government action, the implied incapacity to act would amount to a denial of the sovereignty of any State which claims such permanent sovereignty.[19]

(4) *Foreign Investments.* To claim the right to regulate and exercise authority over foreign investments within the national jurisdiction is the prerogative of any sovereign State. Yet, whether a State may do so "in accordance with its laws and regulations" depends, at least in international law, on the compatibility of these laws and regulations with international law.

In particular, to comply with the international law standard, any interference with foreign investments must be for public purposes only and is subject to the condition of the payment of prompt, effective and full or adequate compensation. Otherwise, irrespective of how the act of interference is termed, lawful expropriation becomes illegal confiscation.

Similarly, the proposition that no State shall be compelled to grant preferential treatment to foreign investments is unobjectionable. Under the United Nations Charter, at least the threat or use of force against a State would make the transaction voidable. Yet, compliance with the international law standard in favour of foreign nationals is not preferential treatment. It is treatment of such nationals in accordance with international law which, irrespective of whether this standard is higher or lower than the national standard, home States are entitled to invoke in favour of their nationals abroad.[20]

(5) *Transnational Companies.* In international law, the right of States under international law to regulate and supervise the activities of any company which operates in its territory is unquestioned. In spite of the recent "discovery" of multinational or transnational companies for purposes of international law and relations, the most suitable tests applicable — registration and control — have been known and applied in international law for a considerable time.[21]

Typical issues arise in cases of alleged international responsibility, especially that of a State in which transnational companies operate. The difficulty is that, in the absence of a test agreed on in any particular case, every State is free to assert or deny the existence of a special link between a claimant State and a transnational company.

In favour of the incorporation test, coupled with that of a special

19 On the Resolution of the General Assembly on Permanent Sovereignty over Natural Resources, adopted December 14, 1962, (1803 - XVII) and subsequent resolutions in a similar vein, see, further, *loc. cit.* above, note 17 (1970), p. 40 *et seq.*

20 See, further, *loc. cit.* above, note 7, p. 3 *et seq.*

21 See, further, *loc. cit.* above, note 1, Vol. I (1957), pp. 387 and 584 *et seq.*, and Vol. II (1968), p. 75 *et seq.*

link between the claimant State and the company concerned, it can at least be said that it has behind it the authority of a recent Judgment of the International Court of Justice.[22] In cases in which the special link with the State of registration appears to be unduly fragile, the control test is likely to yield a workable secondary test. Thus, for purposes of international responsibility, no need for particular types of foreign company appears to exist. What would be helpful would be agreement on the tests applicable for purposes of allocating foreign companies to their home States.

(6) *Primary Commodity Producers.* The right of sovereign States to associate in cartels of primary commodity producers is a matter of their sovereign prerogative, but so is that of consumer States to join in the defence of their own sectional interests.

Under the Charter of Economic Rights and Duties of States, the right of association of producers is to be elevated into an element of the international economic order. Yet, a corresponding right of association is denied to consumer countries. This type of discrimination is unlikely to enhance the chances of a consensual economic order on a basis of "co-operation among all States". It alone would go far to explain some of the abstentions and votes against the adoption of the Resolution.

(7) *Preferential Treatment.* The emphasis in the Charter on generalised non-discriminatory and non-reciprocal preferences in favour of "developing" countries is understandable but not necessarily convincing.

Which of the various standards of international economic law is appropriate in any particular case is a matter of, in the last resort, political judgment on the part of any country involved. Autarkist States or blocks may take one view of the matter towards States associated with them and another towards States with which relations are indifferent if not hostile. Other States may prefer to adhere to standards of reciprocal non-discrimination.

To attempt to elaborate the exploitation of colonial guilt complexes and the quest for bounties into a legal principle appears to run counter to the most fertile working principle behind the evolution of international economic law and organisation: reciprocity.

(8) *Shared Natural Resources.* The use of this term in the Charter is too vague to be acceptable. If what is meant is the exploitation of the natural resources of one country, for instance, in the continental

[22] *I.C.J. Reports 1970,* p. 38 *et seq.* (Barcelona Traction Company case).
See also I. Seidl-Hohenveldern, *Multinational Enterprises and the International Law of the Future,* 29 *Year Book of World Affairs* (1975), p. 301 *et seq.*

shelf in a manner which may adversely affect a neighbouring country, more specific rules appear to be required.

(9) *Indexation of Prices.* The postulated duty of all States to "co-operate in achieving adjustments in the prices of exports of developing countries in relation to prices of their imports so as to promote just and equitable terms of trade for them, in a manner which is remunerative for producers and equitable for producers and consumers"[23] may be questioned on two grounds:

In the first place, is the possibly implied intention to index prices based on the further implied assumption of a chronic and progressive world inflation? If so, the issue closely affects unsolved problems of a more commensurate monetary world order than the International Monetary Fund has to offer, and this can hardly be settled as a question incidental to export prices of "developing" countries.

Secondly, how, without interfering unduly with the sovereign equality of States, is a just and equitable relation to be attained between the export of, for instance, primary products and prestige imports such as the latest weaponry from the arsenals of "developed" countries?

Transcendental Criticism. The inclusion in the fundamental principles of the contemplated international economic order of non-intervention and abstention from hegemonial designs and the creation of spheres of influence is symptomatic. It is indicative of illusions on the relations between international politics and economics.

At least on the international level, economics is a function of politics. Compared with international politics, international economics plays a secondary role, and its scope is decisively conditioned by overriding political considerations.

It is implied in the characterisation of world politics as a system of power politics in disguise that this amounts, at most, to a quasi-order which is based on the unstable equilibrium between the super-Powers and their shared fear of mutual co-extermination. In this environment, to aim at an international economic order in a community sense, as distinct from a quasi-order complementary to the existing political world quasi-order, appears utopian. Thus, as with the General Assembly's definition of aggression, the likely fate of the Charter of Economic Rights and Duties of States is to be used and abused as an ideological weapon.

Constructive Uses. Like other blueprints which are supposed to be applied in an uncongenial environment and, therefore, must remain largely utopian, the Charter of Economic Rights and Duties of States can be put to constructive uses. Each of the items of the Charter which, at successive Sessions, the General Assembly proposes to study in depth

[23] Article 28.

deserves to be examined from the point of view of the obstacles which, in a world system of power politics and power economics in disguise, obstruct its realisation. Such efforts have their educational value: they point to the gulf between aspiration and reality, and, what is even more valuable, they invite reflection on the reasons why.

Beyond this, resolutions such as the Charter of Economic Rights and Duties of States fulfil another unintended but all the more useful function. The voting record of member States serves notice of their political intentions. Votes of countries in favour of the curtailment of existing international law as, for instance, the rules on the protection of foreign investment should, primarily, be taken at their face value. At first sight, none of the capital-importing countries among the one hundred and twenty member States which voted in favour of the Resolution is any longer safe for purposes of *private* investment. This is not to exclude that, on closer investigation, some of these votes may be explicable on acceptable grounds.[24]

Conversely, it would be hasty to assume that abstention from voting or an adverse vote is conclusive evidence of credit-worthiness. It may mean that capital-importing governments in these categories desire to maintain a reasonable climate for private investments or, at least, are shrewd enough not to disclose their hand prematurely.

For members of the General Assembly to realise that their votes have consequences may also assist in imbuing them with a greater sense of responsibility than is manifest so far in the law-making exercises of the General Assembly.

VI — THE DYNAMICS OF INTERNATIONAL LAW AND THE INTERNATIONAL COURT OF JUSTICE

The experience that judges not only find the law but also make and develop it applies as much to international as municipal law. In deciding on the submission of cases to international judicial organs, parties anticipate, within limits, this possibility. Acquiescence by parties in such arrogation of quasi-legislative functions provides a consensual basis for an, otherwise, questionable exercise of jurisdiction by international courts and tribunals. Insofar as third parties are concerned, the authority of awards and judgments of international judicial organs is, in any case, merely persuasive. Thus, acceptance or rejection of controversial judicial interpretations of the law lies in their own hands.

If, in an organised international society, the optional jurisdiction of international judicial organs in contentious cases is supplemented by an advisory judicial jurisdiction, the purpose of this advisory jurisdiction may be what it purports to be: to provide legal guidance to the political organ which requests the advisory opinion. Yet, if the political organ con-

24 See, further, *loc. cit.* above, note 7 (1969), p. 185 *et seq.*

cerned can expect an answer from the Court in line with its policies, it may be tempted to employ advisory proceedings for other ends. For instance, in the case of a drastic change in the composition of a judicial organ, its advisory jurisdiction may be employed to override in fact, if not in law, a previous judgment of a purged Court. Similarly, a political organ may invoke the advisory jurisdiction of a court in order to obtain in this indirect way answers which, in substance, amount to the decision of issues between parties to an actual dispute. While the 1971 *Namibia (South West Africa)* Opinion of the International Court of Justice may be thought to illustrate the first variant,[25] that of the Court on the *Western Sahara* (1975) may be considered as a sophisticated illustration of the second. In playing down the inter-temporal claims of Morocco and the "Mauritanian entity" — whatever this *ex post* invention of the Arab League may be supposed to mean — the Court has opened the door wide to the creation of a pseudo-sovereign entity in line with the decolonisation ideology prevalent in the General Assembly and to hegemonial aspirations of Algeria as *tertius gaudens.*[26]

The Court's Composition

To create conditions of immunity of the Permanent Court of International Justice and the International Court of Justice from outside pressure was one of the objects of the Statutes of both Courts.

In the life-time of the Permanent Court of International Justice, the Advisory Opinion on the *Austro-German Customs Union* (1931) was the chief instance in which the policies of the major European Powers and the votes of the judges of their nationality appeared to coincide miraculously.[27]

In the International Court of Justice, the independence shown by one of the judges in the *Anglo-Iranian Oil Company* case (1952) towards, admittedly, tortuous arguments advanced by his own government was widely and favourably commented upon.[28] As this particular vote tends to be cited in a generalised form, it should be recalled that, in the country involved, the exercise of judicial independence is admired and, so far, not

25 *I.C.J. Reports 1971,* p. 16 *et seq.*

26 *Ibid., 1975,* p. 12 *et seq.*

On the background triangular dispute between Spain, Mauritania and Morocco, primarily concerned with the phosphate mines at Bou Craa, see *The Times* (London), July 8, 1975, and *The Economist,* September 13, 1975, p. 58.

27 A/B 41, p. 37 *et seq.*

See, further, H. Lauterpacht, *The Function of Law in the International Community* (1933), p. 158, note 1, and *The Development of International Law by the Permanent Court of International Justice* (1934), p. 21, and J. H. W. Verzijl's case note (1931), reprinted in *The Jurisprudence of the World Court,* Vol. I (1965), p. 257 *et seq.*

On arbitration awards "suspected of having been given under the influence of other than juridical motives", see Judge Ammoun's Sep. Op. in the *Barcelona Traction Case, I.C.J. Reports 1970,* p. 299.

28 Sep. Op., President Sir Arnold McNair, *I.C.J. Reports 1952,* p. 116 *et seq.*

visited with sanctions which, in more authoritarian regimes, serve to ensure self-co-ordination in high offices abroad.

Factors affecting Election

To be elected, members of the International Court of Justice require a double majority in the Security Council and the General Assembly of the United Nations.[29] Thus, with the exception of the two super-Powers which may be expected not to brook any interference, however mild, with the nomination of their candidates, others may consider it advisable to select their candidates with an eye on the acceptability of their candidates to the international constituencies concerned. Moreover, appointments are for a limited period of nine years,[30] and some judges may desire to be re-elected.

The minimum requirements laid down in the Court's Statute for judges are of moderate stringency and, in a growing practice, judges take their "qualifying examinations" for acceptability to the two political organs of the United Nations in a process of continuous assessment in the Legal Committee of the General Assembly, the International Law Commission, or both of these organs with strong political overtones. The records of candidates in these bodies enable judges of "form" to obtain fairly accurate estimates of the "co-operation" to be expected from judges in the making.

Also, it cannot be easily overlooked that members of the Court from authoritarian and totalitarian States have been conditioned in their home States to view law as a direct instrument of politics and owe to their political reliability their advancement in the politico-legal hierarchies of their home states. Is it likely that, on their transposition to the Court, they are able to accept, otherwise than in the letter, "bourgeois illusions" on the desirability of their self-immunisation from metalegal pressures?

Evidence

The generalisations contained in the preceding Section are based on freely available evidence on the pattern generally adopted by authoritarian and totalitarian systems and on the types of person who, in these systems, tend to climb quickest and highest on the politico-legal ladders or, conversely, are most likely to share the fates of the shadowy figures depicted in Solzhenitsyn's *The First Circle* (1968).

To be fair to the exceptions to these presumptions, more concrete tests must be found and applied impartially to all the members of the Court. In this respect three types of case are especially high-yielding: those in-

29 Articles 4-12, I.C.J. Statute.
See also the evaluation of the Court's electoral system by S. Rosenne, *The Law and Practice of the International Court*, Vol. I (1965), p. 184 *et seq.*

30 Article 13 (1), I.C.J. Statute.

volving consideration of the Purposes and Principles of the United Nations and those concerned with the interpretation of politically sensitive Articles of the Charter.

The Purposes of the United Nations

A growing number of members of the Court have employed at least seven questionable techniques to overcome the limitations of the United Nations Charter on, for instance, the protection of fundamental rights and freedoms of individuals:

(1) Reasoning on lines of a community type of natural law, in disregard of the restraints imposed by Article 38 of the Statute of the International Court of Justice.

(2) Identification of the second and third Purposes of the United Nations or any of its constituent elements with what has been described as the law recognised by the United Nations, a practice accepted as law or general principles of law recognised by civilised nations.

(3) Linking the second and third Purposes with the first and extending the application of the rules available for the implementation of the first Purpose to the other two.

(4) Justification of the binding character of human rights by reliance on the principle of self-defence in the interest of the implementation of the Purposes of the United Nations.

(5) Extension of forms of extraordinary national jurisdiction, as in cases of war crimes or piracy, to action incompatible with the Purposes of the United Nations.

(6) Use of relevant resolutions of the United Nations organs, especially if repeatedly re-affirmed, as cumulative evidence of an evolutionary law of the United Nations.

(7) Assumption of jurisdiction, combined with claims of acquiescence by dissenting minorities and strengthened by evidence of continued membership of dissenters in the Organisation.

From this point of view, the Individual Opinions of Judges Ammoun, Padilla Nervo and Tanaka are especially instructive, and the Court's reasoning in the *Namibia* case (1971) is even more pointed.[31]

[31] For "inside views" of the Court, see Judge Dillard's Address at the 1973 Dinner of the A.S.I.L. *(Proceedings*, p. 296 *et seq.)* and the Special Report by Sir Gerald Fitzmaurice in *Institut de Droit International, Livre du Centenaire* (1973), p. 279, note 192, in which he refers to "the Court's occasional, relatively rare, findings that *are* open to the charge of political subservience" (emphasis in the original). See also *ibid.*, pp. 284-286, and, further, 4 *Israel Y.B. of Human Rights* (1975), p. 11 *et seq.*, or *loc. cit.* above, note 1, Vol. III (1976), Chapters 12-15.

The Principles of the United Nations

Perhaps even more revealing than the treatment meted out by the International Court of Justice to the Purposes is that given to the Principles of the United Nations, the consensual *jus cogens* of the Organisation. From the angle of the dynamics of international law, the attempts made openly by Judge Ammoun and, more discreetly, by the Court to assimilate the principle of equal rights and self-determination of peoples to that of sovereign equality in Article 2 (1) of the United Nations Charter are fascinating.

No less symptomatic is the attempt to read the first half-sentence of Article 2 (5) of the United Nations Charter as if it did not contain the words "in accordance with the present Charter" as a qualification of the duty of member States to give every assistance to the United Nations. This interpretation indicates as much a trend towards a cavalier treatment of safeguards in favour of the sovereignty of member States as the Court's treatment of the rights of non-member States under Article 2 (6) and the freedom of member States from United Nations intervention under Article 2 (7) of the Charter in a process of "ever less strict interpretation".[32]

Politically Sensitive Articles

In interpreting the right of agency of the Security Council under Articles 24 and 25 of the United Nations Charter, the International Court of Justice appears to have erred as much in the direction of an unduly extensive interpretation of the jurisdiction of the Security Council[33] as did a differently composed Court in its affirmation of an almost unlimited right of budgetary control by the General Assembly under Article 17 of the United Nations Charter.[34]

Similarly, the attempts made since 1950 by "progressive" members of the Court to give Article 80 of the United Nations Charter more than its purely negative meaning of a "without prejudice" clause deserve to be recalled.[35] They furnish evidence of the fact that metalegal commitments are not the monopoly of any one quarter, and they confirm the experience that such exercises impair not only the Court's standing but also the quality of judicial reasoning.

VII—THE DOCTRINE OF INTERNATIONAL LAW AND THE DYNAMICS OF INTERNATIONAL LAW

In each of its three principal fields — analysis, synopsis and guidance —

32 Vice-President Ammoun (Sep. Op.), *I.C.J. Reports 1970,* p. 314.
See, further, *loc. cit.* above, note 1, Vol. III (1976), Chapter 20 (2).

33 See, further, *ibid.,* Chapter 25.

34 See, further, *ibid.,* Chapter 27.

35 See, further, *ibid.,* Chapter 28.

the Doctrine of international law can make a distinct contribution of its own to the elucidation of the dynamics of international law.

Analysis

The foremost task of Doctrine must remain that of testing the accuracy of any claim that the dynamics of international law have led to any asserted change of existing international law. Article 38 of the Statute of the International Court of Justice provides a yard-stick which serves the purposes of the Doctrine of international law as much as it does those of the International Court of Justice.

The assertions made by other law-determining agents — States, acting individually or collectively as, for instance, in organs of international institutions, and Courts — regarding supposed changes in international law provide plentiful raw material for continuous assessment and reassessment.

What governments do offers more reliable indications of the trends in international law than what governments say. From this point of view, treaties are an earnest of the optional principles and standards which States are prepared to accept and of the radius within which this law is to operate.

The more other law-determining agencies are in danger of succumbing to extraneous temptations and pressures, the more crucial becomes the function of the Doctrine of international law.[36] This places a special responsibility on international lawyers in the diminishing number of countries which still grant to scholarship an adequate degree of autonomy and freedom of dissent from their local establishments.

Synopsis and Guidance

While, both in its historical and sociological variants, synopsis is inevitably backward-looking, a forward-looking alternative to completely subjective forecasting exists in the field of international planning and legislation. It is to provide a variety of relevant models of international law and order from which future law-makers may take their pick. Such a relativist approach makes it possible to give full vent to the dynamics of international law in the making.

36 See, further, the writer's *The Inductive Approach to International Law* (1965), p. 43 *et seq.*

Chapter 3

HISTORICAL MODELS OF INTERNATIONAL LAW

TOWARDS A COMPARATIVE HISTORY OF INTERNATIONAL LAW

> *"Is not the eye surfeited with seeing, and the ear sated with hearing? What has happened will happen again, and what has been done will be done again, and there is nothing new under the sun. Is there anything of which one can say, 'Look, this is new'? No, it has already existed, long before our time. The men of old are not remembered, and those who follow will not be remembered by those who follow them."* Ecclesiastes 1. 8-11

This Chapter is a plea for a radical re-appraisal of the treatment of the history of international law as a subject of teaching and research.*

It would be tempting to introduce the discussion with a reasonably full and critical historiography of the subject. It must suffice to limit this aspects of the matter to a summary of six phases into which, in rough sequence, the evolution of the history of international law during the last five hundred years may be divided:

(1) Use of more or less well-authenticated mythical and historical material for purposes of illustration.

(2) Identification of the history of international law with that of the history of natural law.

(3) Treatment of the history of international law as evidence of the manifestation of the tenets of revealed religions.

(4) Exposition of the history of international law as part of diplomatic history.

(5) Identification of the history of international law with that of its doctrine.

* In preparing this Chapter, I received unstinted assistance from the staff of the Libraries of the British Museum and University College, especially Miss Delia Bowden and Mr. M. A. Jahn, and, on the illustrations chosen from Egyptian and Hittite practice, I benefited from valuable criticism by Professor V. Korošec, Director of the Institute for Oriental Studies of the Slovene Academy, Ljubliana, Professor H. S. Smith of the Egyptology Department, and Miss M. S. Drower of the Ancient History Department, of University College London.

(6) Change in emphasis from the history of the doctrine to that of State and judicial practice.

In this context, it must also suffice to formulate in positive terms seven *desiderata* of a more commensurate treatment of the history of international law as a branch of public international law and merely to imply criticism of the failings of the six techniques enumerated above.

The study of the history of international law should comply with seven requirements:

(1) It should be conceived as an interdisciplinary subject which applies to the evolution of international law any relevant techniques of social sciences, in particular those of history, international relations (understood as the branch of sociology concerned with international society), social anthropology, economics and jurisprudence (philosophy of law and analytical legal theory).

(2) It should avoid any type of "committed" scholarship or teleology.

(3) It should make the maximal use of relevant background information from different cultural environments.

(4) It should reduce to a minimum any merely chronological or amorphous treatment of the subject.

(5) It should reflect awareness of the rise, plurality and passing of individual civilisations since the dawn of recorded history.

(6) It should be selective, rather than eclectic. Decisions on the inclusion and exclusion of potentially relevant material should be based on explicit criteria, and preference should be given to primary material.

(7) It should be synoptic rather than encyclopaedic.

Before attempting to illustrate techniques which, it may be hoped, will meet the tests postulated, it is necessary to examine a related issue: the problem of continuity and discontinuity in international law.

I—CONTINUITY AND DISCONTINUITY IN INTERNATIONAL LAW

The question of the continuity of international law can be made unnecessarily complicated by two failings: over-estimation of the history of the doctrine of international law, as compared with its practice, and disregard of the dichotomy between international law and order.

Doctrinal Continuity

International law, as it developed during a thousand years of practice in the European chancelleries, owes little to Roman law, and even less to earlier systems of international law, some of which existed more than three thousand years ago. At most, the training of medieval clerks in the Canon Law and of students in the law schools of the Italian post-glossators influenced categories of legal thinking and the terminology employed in the drafting of some of the documents of medieval international practice.

Admittedly, in any view of international law through the eyes of the purported "fathers" of international law and their epigones the story looks different. These largely speculative thinkers and rationalisers of the naturalist period of the doctrine of international law owe as much to the revival of classical literature as to the Judaeo-Christian background of their theological, philosophical, historical and legal education. Yet, this doctrinal continuity hardly establishes a legal continuity between the systems of international law applied in ancient and our days.

Relevant Distinctions

For our purposes, the distinction between law and order in general, and international law and order in particular, is helpful.[1] In this context, it is also advisable to recall the differences between the social infrastructures of highly integrated communities and more loosely organised international societies of the past and present.

Highly integrated communities tend to sublimate their *de facto* orders and reduce them to a position of last resort in emergencies. Normally, they rely on intricate legal systems with sophisticated webs of public and private rights and duties.

In such communities, even political revolutions tend to upset but little the continuity of legal relations in the sphere of private law and subordinate public relations. The case is different with social revolutions, such as the French Revolution of 1789 or the Russian October Revolution of 1917. In upheavals of this nature, private and public law, together with their underlying social structures, may completely vanish.

On the international scene, a central order, comparable to those of national and multinational communities, has as yet failed to materialise. In unorganised international society and confederate international societies on the League of Nations or United Nations pattern, the place of a cen-

1 On the peace treaties concluded between 1648 and 1815 as the basis of European international relations during the various inter-war periods, see U. Scheuner, "Die grossen Friedensschluesse als Grundlage der europaeischen Staatenordnung zwischen 1648 und 1815" in K. Repgen and S. Skalweit (eds.), *Spiegel der Geschichte (Braubach Festgabe*—1964), p. 220 *et seq.*, "Buendnispolitik als Grundlage der europaeischen Friedensordnung," *7 Europa-Archiv* (1971), p. 225 *et seq.*, and, on the relations between international law and its correlated international quasi-orders in general, the present writer's *International Law and Order* (1971), p. 8 *et seq.* See also W. Janssen, *Die Anfaenge des modernen Voelkerrechts und der neuzeitlichen Diplomatie* (1965), p. 84 *et seq.*

tral order is taken by competing alliances, shifting balances of power or other typical devices of international systems of open power politics or power politics in disguise.

Minor or duel wars affect but little these international quasi-orders. By the laws of war and neutrality, international customary law even makes provision for such armed conflicts.

If international quasi-orders, such as the Westphalian Peace Treaties of 1648, the Vienna Peace Treaties of 1815 or the Paris Peace Treaties of 1919, break down, the rules of international customary law which exist at any of these ruptures appear to be little the worse for the destruction of their correlated political and legal frameworks.

The reason lies in the specific character of the rules of international customary law. As distinct from the substantive rules of internal law, the rules of international customary law are largely jurisdictional (those on sovereignty and the freedom of the seas), enabling (those on consent, recognition and self-defence), relativising (those on good faith) or complementary to these rules (those on international responsibility).

In any international quasi-order established after a major war, fairly stereotyped needs call for rules of international customary law similar to those which were applied in the preceding pre-war period. The reason is that, more likely than not, the new post-war order rests on another system of open power politics or power politics in disguise.

The breaks in the international quasi-orders of any inter-war period are real enough. If, as in 1815, 1919 and 1945, the challengers of the pre-war *status quo* are defeated, truncated or eliminated, these breaks are less apparent. Especially is this true if, by and large, the victors are content to re-establish and confirm the previous post-war international quasi-order in the peace settlements. That such continuity, retrospectively re-established, is purely fortuitous becomes evident from a comparison of the actual with a hypothetical situation: the victory, in any of these cases, of those who actually happened to be defeated. However much their victory might have changed the international quasi-order of the post-war period in question, victorious challengers of the pre-war *status quo* would probably have invoked for their own purposes most of the pre-war rules of international customary law.

This discrepancy between the discontinuity in international quasi-orders and the continuing need for the devices of international customary law explains the limited relevance of any particular peace settlement of the last few hundred years as the supposed starting point of contemporary international law.

Such importance as the actual continuity of any particular international quasi-order or rule of international law—treaty law or international customary law—may claim is likely to be related to problems of inter-temporal international law, the ascertainment of the binding character of a particular treaty and the verification of the significance of the evidence produced in favour of an asserted rule of international customary law.[2]

For a deeper understanding of international law—and as a potential pattern of international legislation in our own time—the continued existence of any particular system of international law or any of its rules is immaterial. What matters is whether any such systems or rules represent models which correspond to present-day needs or show failings which are more clearly discernible at a distance than in a contemporary setting.

II—FIVE MODELS OF INTERNATIONAL LAW

The object of the models approach to the history of international law is to present a comprehensive and accurate, if simplified, picture of the historical reality of international law.[3]

The distinguishing feature of each model is the system of inter-locking rules which pertain to it.

To emphasise how little typical requirements of sovereign States have changed over the centuries, if not millennia, preference will be given in the illustration of the models to be presented in this Chapter to older rather than more recent material. If such material pertains to international societies which have vanished long ago, its persuasive value is even greater. Irrespective of any alleged legal continuity, it attests to the recurrent needs of sovereign States in environments which are governed primarily by power, rather than community motivations.

Five models of international law will serve to illustrate why international customary law is so little affected by the breakdown of any particular international quasi-order: (1) the omnipotence model; (2) the *jus strictum* model; (3) the *jus aequum* model; (4) the oceanic model; (5) the unionist model.

(1) *Model of Omnipotence*

Territorial supremacy can be attained on a purely *de facto* basis. It may be exercised by a universal State or a plurality of States which claim supremacy over particular areas, exercise reasonably effective control over these

[2] See, for instance, the Pleadings before the International Court of Justice in the *Minquiers and Ecrehos* case (1953) between France and the United Kingdom, relying on the Anglo-French Treaties of 1217, 1259, 1360 and 1420 (Vol. I, pp. 142 *et seq.* and 602); the discussions on Gibraltar between Spain and the United Kingdom, turning, *inter alia,* on the interpretation of Article X of the Peace Treaty of Utrecht of 1713 (Spanish Ministry of Foreign Affairs, *Red Book* on Gibraltar (1965), p. 13 *et seq.*, and United Kingdom, Cmnd. 3131 (1966), p. 8 *et seq.*, and the judgment of the French *Cour de Cassation* of March 22, 1960, in *Moss* v. *Procureur Général près la Cour d'Appel de Paris,* relying on the Treaty of December 8, 1805, between Napoleon I and the Elector of Baden, in which the secret clauses of an earlier Treaty of August 25, 1796, between the same parties were confirmed (40 *International Law Reports,* 50 at p. 51).

[3] On the models approach to international law in general, see *International Law and Order, loc. cit.* above, note 1, p. 252 *et seq.*

For a typology, based on differences in the organisation of the constituent elements of international legal systems, see Paul Vinogradoff, *Historical Types of International Law, Bibliotheca Visseriana,* Vol. I (1923), p. 3 *et seq.*

areas and, within them, deny equality of status to any competitor.

Leaving aside peripheral treaty commitments on a footing of legal equality, the claim made by Lugalannemundu, King of Sumer (perhaps about 2600 B.C.), to "kingship over the whole world," the Roman Empire and imperial China—the "Middle" Kingdom—at the summit of their power illustrate this model and the possibility of the co-existence of a plurality of universalist, if not universal, States.[4]

The external public law, applied by the early Roman republic as part of its *jus fetiale*[5] to, for instance, the declaration of war on foreign States, or the concept of international law as "*aeusseres Staatsrecht*" (foreign public law) are other legal manifestations of this pattern.

In a letter from the Great Khan Gueyuek (1246—48) to Pope Innocent IV, the substance of the argument is uncompromisingly stated:

> "Thanks to the power of the Everlasting Heaven, all lands have been given to us from sunrise to sunset. How could anyone act otherwise than according to the Command of Heaven? Now you must say with upright heart: We will be your subjects and will place our powers at your disposal. You in person at the head of the monarchs, all of you without exception, must come to tender us service and pay us homage: then only will we recognise your submission. But if you do not obey the Command of Heaven and run counter to our orders, we shall know that you are our foe. That is what we have to tell you. If you fail

4 S. N. Kramer, *The Sumerians* (1963), pp. 51—52.

When the 13000 tablets, written in Sumeric and a, so far, unknown language in the State archive of Ebla (south of Aleppo) have been deciphered, further exciting evidence on international law in the period between 2350 and 2250 B.C. is likely to emerge. For a preliminary report on the excavations under the leadership of Professor Matthiae (Rome), see *The Times* (London), October 31, 1975, p.7.

On the Roman model of imperial universality, as distinct from frequently less ambitious practices, see, for instance, Virgil, *Aeneid,* VI, 851-853 (Appeal of Anchises to Aeneas, father of the Romans).

On the Chinese model of universality, see the Mandate of 1793, by the Emperor of China, Chien Lung, in response to a letter from King George III of England (Frederick Whyte, *China and Foreign Powers* (1928), p. 41), and, on the economic relations between China and the Roman Empire, L. Boulnois, *La Route de la Soie* (1963), Chap. 2 *et seq.*

For Roman and Chinese practices based on the consensual model (see under II (3)), see A. Heuss, *Die voelkerrechtlichen Grundlagen der roemischen Aussenpolitik in republikanischer Zeit* (1933); H. Bengston, *Die Vertraege der griechisch-roemischen Welt von 700 bis 338 v. Chr.* (1962); Shih-tsai Chen, *The Equality of States in Ancient China*, 35 A.J.I.L. (1941), p. 641 *et seq.*, and R.L. Walker, *The Multi-State System of Ancient China* (1953).

5 See, further, C. Phillipson, *The International Law and Custom of Ancient Greece and Rome* (1911), Vol. II, p. 315 *et seq.*; P. Willems, *Le Droit Public Romain* (1910), p. 343, note 3; and A. Burdese, *Manuale di Diritto Pubblico Romano* (1966), p. 101 *et seq.*

In the palace of Khusro I Anoshirwan at Ctesiphon (on the River Euphrates thirty-five miles north of Baghdad—sixth century A.D., three empty seats stood below the royal throne. They were for the emperor of China, the great khagan (ruler of the nomads in Central Asia) and the Roman emperor if they should ever come as vassals to the court of the King of Kings of the Sassanian empire (P. Brown, *The World of Late Antiquity* (1971), p. 160).

to act in accordance with it, how can we foresee what will happen to you? Heaven alone knows."[6]

(2) *Jus Strictum Model*

This model presupposes the co-existence of at least two entities each of which refuses to subordinate itself to the other. Such relations may exist on a *de facto* basis of peaceful or warlike armed co-existence, or the two entities may decide to recognise each other as sovereign and equal in status.

Thus, the Declaration of Arbroath of 1320, embodied in a Petition from the Barons of Scotland to Pope John XXII at Avignon, contains Scotland's request to be treated by England on a footing of sovereign equality.

Leaving aside legendary presentations of Scots history, the Scots claim made in the Declaration rests on two grounds: that the Scots had held Scotland "free of all bondage" ever since their conquest of these parts of the British Isles, and that they merely wished to live in peace with England and coveted nothing but their own.[7]

In accordance with this Petition, the Pope vainly urged Edward II of England to make peace with the Scots. In a letter written in 1324, the Pope addressed Robert Bruce as king and thus recognised him in this capacity. In 1328, Edward III followed suit and recognised Robert Bruce as King of Scotland and the independence of Scotland.[8]

[6] English translation (from Mongol into Persian and from Persian into Latin) in E.D. Phillips, *The Mongols* (1969), p. 82.

As Dr. Phillips was kind enough to inform me, the Persian translation was found in 1922 in a collection of papers, called *Archiva de Castelle,* in the Vatican Library. The Latin translation is available in 32 *Monumenta Germaniae Historiae* (1913), p. 207, and P. Palliat, "Les Mongols et la papauté," 23 *Revue de l'Orient Chrétien* (1923), pp. 13-14.

For another English translation of this letter, see M. Prawdin, *The Mongol Empire* (1940), p. 280 *et seq.*

See also the reply by Great Khan Mangu (1251-1259) to the King of France: "When, by the power of the Eternal God, the whole world from sunrise to sunset has been unified in happiness and in peace, then it will become plain what we shall have to do" *(ibid.* p. 302).

[7] For the Latin text and English translations, see Lord Cooper of Culross, *Selected Papers 1922-1954* (1957), p. 324 *et seq.*, W. C. Dickinson and Others, *A Source Book of Scottish History,* Vol. I (1952), p. 131 *et seq.,* or the facsimile edition, published by H.M. Stationery Office (1969).

On the Declaration, see, further, R. K. Hannay, *The Barons of Scotland to Pope John XXII in 1320* (1936); J. R. Philip, "Sallust and the Declaration of Arbroath," 26 *Scottish Historical Review* (1947), pp. 75-78, and Lord Cooper, *loc. cit.* above, p. 324 *et seq.*

[8] The changes of English policy regarding the recognition of Robert Bruce as King of Scotland are instructive.

In a letter of August 3, 1309, from King Edward II to King Philip IV of France, Edward II enclosed two letters which Mahen de Varennes, emissary of the French King, carried with him, and which were addressed to Robert Bruce. While the letter which Varennes carried openly was addressed to Sir Robert Bruce as Earl of Carryk, the other letter which was secreted in his belt was addressed to Robert Bruce as King of Scotland *(Treaty Rolls*—ed. P. Chaplais), Vol. I (1234-1325), No. 472.

In a letter from Pope John XXII of September 15, 1320, to King Edward II (Rymer's *Foedera,* Vol. 3, p. 848, and G. Donaldson, "The Pope's Reply to the Scottish Barons in

Continued on next Page

If, as the documentary evidence available suggests, these acts were intended to be legally relevant, they presuppose a minimal, and rather static, system of international law, consisting of three basic rules:

(1) Any claim to territorial sovereignty must rest on firm possession of a reasonably defined territory and absence of submission, voluntary or otherwise, to any other sovereign.

(2) Recognition of this status may be requested from and granted by other sovereigns.

(3) Request for such recognition necessarily implies recognition as sovereign of the entity from which recognition is sought.

In an embryonic form this model also presupposes some rules on international responsibility in cases of interference with sovereign rights or acts incompatible with recognition. In this type of international society, war is not only a self-understood means of self-defence and, in the absence of obligations to the contrary, an admissible form of offensive but also a background threat, which encourages sovereign States to treat international obligations as more than merely morally binding commitments. The *jus strictum* model also tends to call for some consensual undertakings, such as truces and armistices, and good faith, at least in its minimal and negative meaning of excluding perfidy *(dolus).*

(3) *Jus Aequum Model*

Relations between England and Scotland since the twelfth century A.D. provide ample material to illustrate not only the *jus strictum* model, but

Continued from previous Page

1320," 29 *Scottish Historical Review* (1950), pp. 119-120), Robert Bruce was described as "*Brus, qui pro Scotiae Rege se gerit,*" and, in a letter of April 1, 1324 (*ibid.* Vol. 4, p. 46), Edward II protested against the Pope's contemplated recognition of Robert Bruce as King of Scotland.

In the Truce of May 30, 1323 *(ibid.* Vol. 3, p. 1022), Robert Bruce was described as "Sir Robert de Bruce," but in the document in which Bruce declared his acceptance of the Truce (June 7, 1323, *ibid.* p. 1031), he was styled, towards the end, as "*Roi d'Escoce.*"

In English State papers, the description of Robert Bruce remained fairly constant until 1327. He was referred to as *Robertus de Bruys suique complices et fautores* (see King Edward III's letter of February 15, 1327—*ibid.* Vol. 4, p. 256). In the letter of March 4, 1327 *(ibid.* p. 270), this style was changed to *Robertus de Brus et deputandi ab eo.* In the letter of February 15, 1328 *(ibid.* p. 336), this became *Robertus de Brus ac nobiles de Scotia,* and in the Quitclaim by King Edward III of March 1, 1328, which forms part of the Treaty of Edinburgh of March 17, 1328 (ratified on the English side at the Parliament of Northampton—May 4, 1328), the metamorphosis is completed: *"magnificus princeps dominus Robertus dei gratia rex Scotorum illustris confederatus ac amicus noster"* (E. L. G. Stones (ed.), *Anglo-Scottish Relations 1179-1328* (1965), p. 161).

See also the renunciation of all English claims to supremacy over Scotland, March 1, 1328 (Rymer's *Foedera,* Vol. 4, pp. 337-338); *Calvin's Case* (1608) 2 St.Tr. 559, at pp. 649-650, and, for helpful surveys of earlier Anglo-Saxon relations, Stones, *loc. cit.*, p. 2 *et seq.;* G. W. S. Barrow, *Feudal Britain* (1956), p. 123 *et seq.*, and *Robert Bruce and the Community of the Realm of Scotland* (1965), and A. M. Mackenzie, *Robert Bruce King of Scots* (1966) p. 287 *et seq.*

also the *jus aequum* model and subsequent models.[9] Yet to drive home the potentialities of the models technique and provide further evidence of the wealth of available material, it is advisable to go back two further millennia and exemplify the *jus aequum* model by a treaty of the thirteenth century B.C.

This is the Treaty (now variously dated 1284—83 or 1270—69 B.C.)[10] between King Ramesses II of Egypt and the Hittite King Hattušiliš III for the establishment of eternal peace and good brotherhood between the two rulers as Great Kings and their countries.

For three reasons, it will be advisable to treat this Treaty in greater detail than, at first sight, might appear necessary in the context of a study of models. *First,* the consensual variant of the *jus aequum* model is potentially more significant than any other of the historical models; for it permits drastic changes in international societies to be attained in organic ways. *Secondly,* this particular treaty is fairly comprehensive. Thus, it offers an early illustration of various fields in which allies or States between which a relatively lasting equilibrium has been achieved may be expected to co-operate. *Thirdly,* this treaty of eternal peace and brotherhood is a prototype of others of its genre in subsequent international systems of power politics.

(a) *Treaty texts*

As recorded in the Treaty, which may have been concluded at Kadesh (or Quadesh—north of Damascus), the original was engraved on a silver tablet. So far, this has not come to light. What have survived are cuneiform clay tablets and hieroglyphic inscriptions of the Treaty. The cuneiform version, found in 1906 at the site of the Hittite capital Hattusas (Bogvazkoey, Central Turkey), is written in Akkadian, the diplomatic language of the time in the Eastern Mediterranean.[11] The original text may well have

9 Thus, the Anglo-Scots Peace Treaty of 1328 (see above, note 8) illustrates the *jus aequum* model.

Similarly, the Treaty of 1174 between King Henry II of England and King William I of Scotland (1165-1214), in which, as a prisoner, the latter agreed to become the liegeman of Henry II (Rymer's *Foedera,* Vol. 1, p. 39; Stones, *loc. cit.* above, note 8, p. 2 *et seq.,* and A. A. M. Duncan, "The Earliest Scottish Charters," 37 *Scottish Historical Review* (1958), p. 103 *et seq.*) exemplifies the version of the consensual model on a footing of inequality between the contracting parties (see, further, below under *Model 5*). See also the Declaration made by King William I in 1189 and his letter of February or March 1214 to King John of England in G. H. Barrow and W. W. Scott (eds.), *Regesta Regum Scottorium,* Vol. II (1971), pp. 309-310 and 456-457 and below, pp. 59-60.

10 See, for instance, V. Korošec, *Hettitische Staatsvertraege* (1931), who dates the Treaty as 1292-1291 B.C. (p. 5—see also *ibid.* p. 58, note 8); W. Helck, *Die Beziehungen Aegyptens zu Vorderasian im 3. und 2. Jahrtausend* (1962), p. 199 *et seq.,* who prefers the date of 1270 (p. 224). See also below, note 14.

11 See, further, A. Meillet and M. Cohen, *Les Langues du Monde* (1952), Vol. I, p. 99 *et seq.,* and S. Langdon and Alan H. Gardiner, "The Treaty of Alliance between Hattusilis, King of the Hittities, and the Pharaoh Ramesses II of Egypt," *6 Journal of Egyptian Archaeology*

Continued on next Page

been drafted in Akkadian and settled by a mixed commission of representatives of the two parties.[12] The hieroglyphic inscriptions on the *stelae,* one erected in the temple of Karnak and the other in the Ramesseum, the mortuary temple of Ramesses II, are probably Egyptain translations, suitably edited to flatter the Pharaoh, of the Akkadian original.[13]

(b) *Interpretation*

In interpreting treaties of this type, it is advisable to remember that the international lawyer who, like the present writer, is not a trained linguist in these ancient languages must, of necessity, rely on translations of these texts. Moreover, even the clay tablets and inscriptions of the treaty used by historians of the period are merely translations of lost originals, and these translations are partly restored and to this extent, at best, inspired guesswork.

At the same time, some of these restorations are based on stereotyped phrases, also found in other treaties of a similar type and of the same period, and can be accepted as near-certainties. Moreover, the political background of international relations in systems of power politics is remarkably stable. Thus, interpretations based on the assumption of mixed

[12] See Helck, *loc. cit.* above, note 10, p. 24.

In 1969, the Turkish Government presented a facsimile version of the Akkadian text of the Treaty to the United Nations.

For a German translation of the Akkadian text of the Treaty, supplemented by the Egyptian translation, see E. F. Weidner, *Politische Dokumente aus Kleinasien (Boghazköi-Studien,* ed. by O. Weber, Nos. 8 and 9, 1923—reprinted 1970), p. 113 *et seq.*

For all purposes other than controversial issues, the English translation of this text by A. Goetze in J. B. Pritchard (ed.), *Ancient Near Eastern Texts* (1969), p. 201 *et seq.*, has been used in this Chapter.

[13] See Helck, *loc. cit.* above, note 10, p. 224.

For the Egyptian text and a German translation, see W. M. Mueller, *Der Buendnisvertrag Ramses II und des Chetiterkoenigs, Mitteilungen der vorderasiatischen Gesellschaft* (1902, 5), p. 193 *et seq.*, and J. A. Wilson in Pritchard, *loc. cit.* above, note 12, p. 199 *et seq.*

Thus, in the inscription on the Treaty at the temple of Abu Simbel, Ramesses II is described as the "smiter of the land of Kheta, which is made of heaps of dead" (J. H. Braested, *Ancient Records of Egypt,* Vol. III (1906), p. 174).

For synoptic translations of both the cuneiform and hieroglyphic versions, see Langdon and Gardiner, *loc. cit.* above, note 11, p. 186 *et seq.*

See, further, B. Porter and R.L.B. Moss, *Topographical Bibliography of Ancient Egyptian Hieroglyphic Texts, Reliefs and Paintings,* Vol. II (1929), p. 49 (2nd ed. in preparation).

Continued from previous Page

(1920), p. 180; *Cambridge Ancient History,* revised eds. of Vols. I and II (1962), Chap. 6 (W. C. Hayes—Chronology, pp. 3, 19-20 and 77-78), and *ibid.* (3rd ed. (1970—eds. I. E. S. Edwards, C. J. Gadd and N. G. L. Hammond), Chronology, p. 173 *et seq.*, at p. 190); M. B. Rowton, "Comparative Chronology at the Time of Dynasty XIX," 19 *Journal of Near Eastern Studies* (1960), p. 15 *et seq.;* E. Hornung, "Untersuchungen zur Chronologie und Geschichte des Neuen Reiches," *Aegyptologische Abhandlungen,* Vol. II (1964) and D. Lorton, *The Juridical Terminology of International Relations in Egyptian Texts through Dyn. XVIII* (1974).

On Akkadian and the cuneiform script, see also S. N. Kramer, *loc. cit.* above, note 4, pp. 18-19.

motivations governing players in eristic environments are unlikely to go far wrong.

(c) *Political background*

Egypt and Hatti had been involved in a prolonged and costly war against each other over the control of Syria and fought an indecisive major battle at Kadesh. The date of the battle is now thought to be either 1300—1299 or 1286—1285 B.C.[14] What is reasonably certain is that, at this point, an equilibrium between the Egyptian and Hittite Empires had been achieved. The minor kings and towns in what, in our time, would be Syria and Lebanon, remained tributaries of Hatti, and those of Palestine fell under Egyptian control. The rising threat of Assyria in the east and the accession to the Hittite throne of a new king, Hattušiliš III, provided further inducements for a lasting settlement between the parties.[15]

(d) *Contracting parties*

The Kings of Egypt and Hatti were the primary parties to the Treaty. The heirs of each king were associated with the Treaty as "brothers like us." It was also made clear that these relations existed not only between the two monarchs in a personal capacity but extended to their countries as a whole—in a more recent terminology, that these heads of State represented their countries: "and as for the relationship of the land of Egypt with the Hatti land, they are at peace and brothers like us forever."

The two kings recognised each other as "great kings," to distinguish themselves from the vassals and tributary princes on both sides,[16] and as brothers, that is, as equals in status.

14 See, for instance, Langdon and Gardiner, *loc. cit.* above, note 11, pp. 202-203, V. Korošec, *loc. cit.* above, note 10, p. 82, and 23 *Sammelband wissenschaftlicher Abhandlungen* (1950), published by the Faculty of Laws, University of Ljubliana (summary in an English translation of a paper on "International Relations according to Cuneiform Records from the Tall Al-Amarna and Hittite State Archives"), p. 39, and "The Warfare of the Hittites from the Legal Point of view," 25 *Iraq* (1963), p. 159 *et seq.;* Helck, *loc. cit.* above, note 10, p. 211 *et seq.;* E. Koenig, "Zum Voelker- und Kriegsrecht im Altertum," 11 *Zeitschriftfuer Voelkerrecht* (1920), p. 167 *et seq.,* and above, note 10.

15 See, further, Braested, *loc. cit.* above, note 13, Vol. III, p. 123 *et seq.,* and *A History of Egypt* (1941), p. 399 *et seq.;* Helck, *loc. cit.* above, note 10, p. 199 *et seq.;* O. R. Gurney, *The Hittites* (1952), pp. 104 and 219 *et seq.;* W. Preisner, "Zum Voelkerrecht der vorklassischen Antike," 4 *Archiv des Voelkerrechts* (1954), pp. 282-283; M. B. Rowton, "The Background of the Treaty between Ramesses II and Hattusilis III," 13 *Journal of Cuneiform Studies* (1959), p. 1 *et seq.;* A. B. Bozeman, *Politics and Culture in International History* (1960), p. 27 *et seq.;* on the Hittites and Syria between 1300 and 1200 B.C., *Cambridge Ancient History,* rev. eds. of Vols. I and II, Chap. XXIV (1965—A. Goetze), p. 40 *et seq.,* and, on Assyrian political and military power during this period, *ibid.* Chap. XXV (1967—J. M. Munn-Rankin), p. 3 *et seq.,* and "Diplomacy in Western Asia in the Early Second Millennium B.C.," 18 *Iraq* (1956), p. 68 *et seq.*

16 See also below under (5).

While Hatti was organised on a feudal basis, Egypt was ruled as an absolutist State, but had tributary princes on its fringes, especially in the borderland of Syria.

INTERNATIONAL LAW AND ORDER CONTENTS OF THE HISTORICAL MODELS

Model *Order* *Fundamental Principles of International Customary Law*

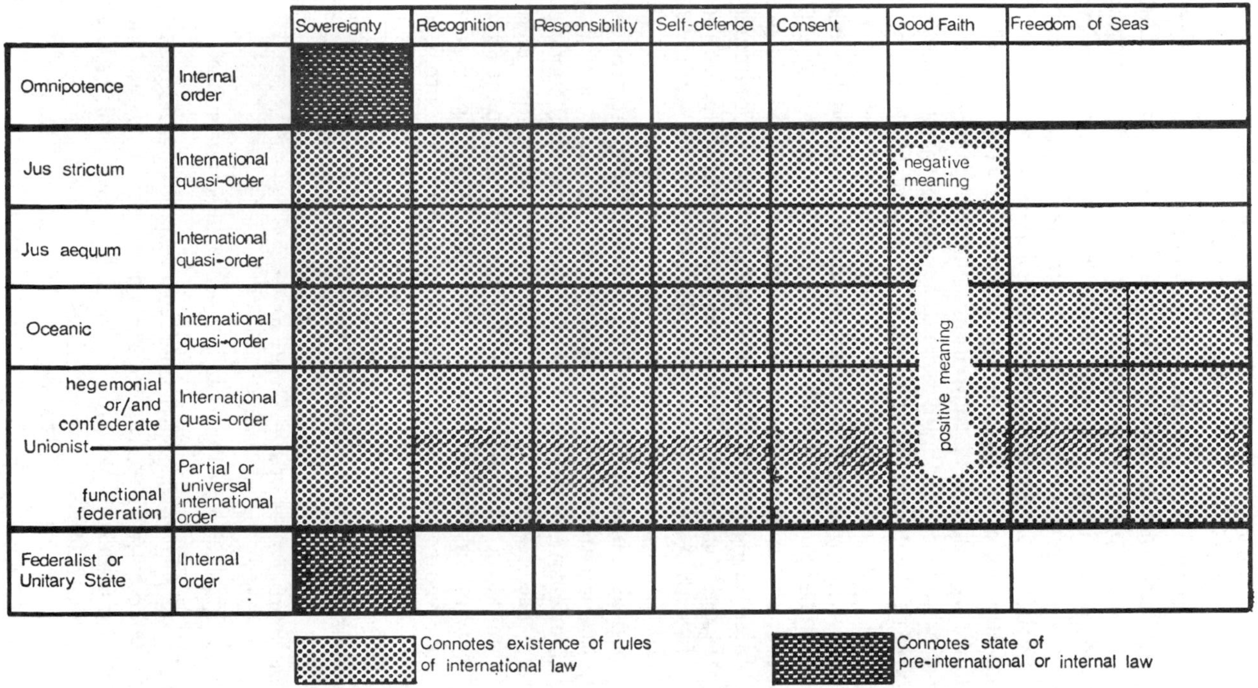

(e) *Objects of the Treaty*

The primary object of the Treaty was to establish a state of lasting peace, as distinct from a mere truce, between the two countries. The repeated emphasis in the Treaty on the brotherhood between all concerned supports the thesis that the term was intended to convey more than equality of status of the primary Contracting Parties. Like the emphasis on the duration of the Treaty "forever," this brotherhood was to express the closeness of relations between the two empires. This friendship was cemented further by the incorporation in the Treaty of stipulations regarding mutual non-aggression, a defensive alliance between the two countries, assistance against rebels, support for the legitimate succession to the throne, extradition of fugitives, and, subsequently, the marriage of the daughter of the Hittite King to the Pharaoh of Egypt as the Queen of Egypt, and not merely as one of his concubines.

The question whether the Treaty should be classified as a peace treaty or an alliance appears to be pointless. In the absence of treaties to the contrary, States were in a state of war. An alliance presupposed a peace treaty and, unless such a treaty led to an alliance, it was only of limited interest. Thus, the Egyptian-Hittite Treaty was both a treaty of peace and alliance, probably with Assyria as the potential common enemy in mind. As in comparable relations of medieval international law,[17] rulers concluded a treaty of peace only if all major issues between them had been settled, or if the parties had an overriding joint interest: a common enemy. In the last case, an offensive or defensive alliance was the natural concomitant of a state of peace between two States in an eristic international environment.

The limitation of the alliance to a defensive alliance in the Egyptian-Hittite Treaty meant that, in any offensive and, usually, predatory war, the party involved could not count on the support of the other contracting party. In contrast, treaties concluded by the Hittite kings with vassals included regularly an obligation of the vassal to participate not only in defensive but also in offensive wars.[18]

(f) *The main clauses of the Treaty*

Some of the clauses of the Treaty deserve closer attention:

(i) *Eternal peace.* The parties agree to "establish good peace and good brotherhood between us for ever. He is a brother to me and I am a brother to him and at peace with him forever." Moreover, this eternal brotherhood covers their heirs and countries.

[17] See, further, the present writer's *The Frontiers of International Law* (1962), p. 96 *et seq.* See also below, text to note 36.

[18] See, further, J. Friedrich, "Staatsvertraege des Hatti Reiches in hettitischer Sprache," 31 *Mitteilungen der Vorderasiatisch-Aegyptischen Gesellschaft* (1926, 1) and 34 *ibid.* (1930, 1), and Korošec, *loc. cit.* above, note 14, p. 72 *et seq.*

Apparently, a logical difficulty presented itself in formulating the objective of eternal peace.[19] If peace was to exist for ever, it ought to have existed in the past. The flaw in this respect is admitted in a masterly understatement: the brotherhood and peace brought about by the Treaty "will be better than the brotherhood and the peace which existed formerly for the land of Egypt with the Hatti land," probably under earlier treaties between the two countries.

The draftsmen did not leave matters at this. With the help of the chief gods on both sides—the Egyptian Sun God and the Hittite Storm God—and a bold religious or legal fiction, they rectified history retrospectively and extended the validity of the Treaty backwards into eternity: "Behold, as for the relationship between the land of Egypt and the Hatti land, since eternity the god does not permit the making of hostility between them because of a treaty valid for ever." Thus, this relationship is deemed to have been "valid since eternity."

(ii) *Non-aggression.* In separate and complementary clauses, the parties agree not to "trespass" into each other's countries nor "take anything therefrom in the future."

(iii) *Defensive alliance.* "If an enemy from abroad comes against the Hatti land or Egypt, and the King of the invaded country" sends to me saying: "Come to me to help me against him," the other Contracting Party "shall send his foot soldiers and his charioteers and they shall slay his enemy and take revenge upon him." *Casus foederis* is formulated so as to leave the decision on the invocation of the Treaty with the injured party.

(iv) *Assistance against rebels.* It is likely that the term "servants belonging to him" includes any rebels against the royal authority of one of the Contracting Parties, including vassals and tributary rulers,[20] and is not limited to subjects, serfs or slaves in the narrower meaning of the term "servants." In any case, the amount of help promised is on the same scale as in the case of an invasion from abroad. Thus, what the parties had in mind was perhaps the scope and seriousness of the rebellion rather than its source.

(v) *Succession to the throne.* In the cuneiform text the clause relating to Hatti land only is preserved, and the corresponding provision concerning Egypt is lost in a gap.

In the case of a threat to the succession of the son of the King of Hatti from the noblemen of the Hatti land, the King of Egypt "shall send foot soldiers and charioteers to take revenge upon them."

In accordance with experiences throughout the ages with invited foreign armed forces, it is expressly stipulated that "after they have

[19] See also Korošec, *loc. cit.* above, note 10, pp. 61-62.
[20] See above, note 16.

re-established order in the country of the King of the Hatti, they shall return to the country of Egypt."

(vi) *Extradition of fugitives.* A careful distinction is drawn in the Treaty between noblemen and other men. In the Egyptian translation, the former are described as prominent persons and the others as persons "whom one does not know."[21]

If a nobleman flees from Hatti and comes to the King of Egypt "in order to enter his services," the King of Egypt shall seize him and have him brought back to Hatti. In the corresponding clause, embodying the duties of the King of Hatti, these duties exist irrespective of whether the nobleman intends to offer his services to the King of Hatti.

It is possible that this omission is merely due to a shorter formulation of this second and complementary clause. Yet in view of the strictly reciprocal formulation of the other main clauses of the Treaty, it may be that this diversity is intentional. The rulers of Hatti were known to make important refugees welcome in their country.[22] Thus, the intention of the parties may have been to formulate the duty of the King of Hatti more widely than that of the King of Egypt. The relative power position speaks, however, against such an interpretation. At the time of the drafting and conclusion of the Treaty, the political and military balance of power appears to have been in favour of Hatti. All that is possible is to point out the textual discrepancy as one open to different interpretations.

If other men—one, two or three—flee from the country of one of the Contracting Parties and "come" to the King of the other country, the same duties of seizure and return of the fugitives apply.

The emphasis in all four clauses on "coming" may indicate that the King of the receiving country is under no obligation to institute searches for fugitives of whose whereabouts in his country he is ignorant.[23] The corresponding formulations of clauses relating to fugitives in treaties between Hittite kings and their vassals, who are bound to facilitate the journeys of such fugitives to the Hittite king,[24] support such a restrictive interpretation.

The significance of the distinction between fugitive noblemen and others becomes apparent from the treatment they are to receive on being returned to their ruler. On the fate of noblemen in this category there is eloquent silence. In the case of other fugitives it is stated in two parallel clauses that the Contracting Parties "are verily brothers; hence let them not exact punishment for their sins, let them not tear out their eyes; let them not take revenge upon their people, together with their wives and with their children."

21 See Mueller, *loc. cit.* above, note 13, pp. 208-209, and Pritchard, *loc. cit.* above, note 12, p. 200, note 14.

22 See, further, Weidner, *loc. cit.* above, note 12, p. 23, note 4.

23 See Mueller, *loc. cit.* above, note 13, p. 229.

24 See, for instance, the Treaty between King Mursilis II of Hatti and Duppi-Tesup of Amarra. concluded between 1355 and 1325 B.C. (Friedrich, *loc. cit.* above, note 18 (1926), p. 21).

In the Egyptian translation, these clauses on fugitives are relegated to a postscript. Even so they form part of the Treaty. It should also be mentioned that it is possible to read the postscript in such a way as to let it apply to both fugitive noblemen and other fugitives.

In any case, what is puzzling is the reason given for these possibly humanitarian provisions. They are derived from the brotherhood or community relations, established between the Contracting Parties.

It has been suggested that the reason for this immunity clause is emphasis on the sovereignty of the Contracting Parties. Yet, perhaps, this view of the matter is too modernistic. In any case, the immunity of fugitives from punishment does not extend to fugitive noblemen. It is also possible to argue that all that is excluded is corporal punishment and mutilation of the returned fugitives, but not their imprisonment or reduction in status to serfdom or slavery.

It may also be that the Contracting Parties looked more pragmatically at the issue. As with the *ne exeat regno* rule in medieval England,[25] it was discontented noblemen, and not the small fry, who constituted a threat to the security of the realm and throne. In the case of traders, artisans or other migrants, clemency could also be shrewd use of skilled manpower, and why should we assume that humanitarianism on the cheap had not its uses then as it has now? Irrespective of whether the clause excluded or included noblemen, it could always be used in two ways. By complying with a request for extradition, a Contracting Party would oblige his counterpart. At the same time, he was able to assuage any powerful friends of returned fugitives by pointing to the immunity clause stipulated in their favour.

(g) *Binding character and sanctions*

Ultimately, the binding character of the Treaty rests on non-legal foundations: a thousand gods invoked by each Contracting Party as the

[25] Under the early English common law, the Crown could prevent any subject from leaving the country (Writ *ne exeat regno*). In the Constitutions of Clarendon (1164) it was more specifically provided that no person, especially not clergy of rank, should leave the realm without the King's licence. Those who were allowed to leave should pledge themselves, if required, not to contrive any hurt to the King or Kingdom during their absence (Cap. IV—W. Stubbs, *Select Charters* (9th ed.—ed. by H. W. C. Davis, 1913), p. 165).

In the Runnymede version of Magna Carta, accepted by King John (June 15, 1215), the King's right to prevent English subjects from leaving the country was limited to times of war (Art. 42), but in King Henry III's First Charter, Article 42 was omitted. See further, Th. P. Taswell-Langmead (ed. Th. F. T. Plucknett), *English Constitutional History* (1946), p. 100.

On the confiscation of passports held by United Kingdom mercenaries returning from Angola to the United Kingdom, see "Ne exeat regno" back again (The Times (London)), February 20, 1976.

Similarly, nobody could abjure his country, nor the allegiance which he owed his country *(Nemo patriam in qua natus est exuere nec ligeantiae debitum ejurare possit* (Coke on Littleton, 129a). See also Justinian, Cod. 10, 38, 4).

On extradition clauses in early English treaties, see P. O'Higgins, "The History of Extradition in British Practice, 1174-1794" *(Indian Year Book of International Affairs 1964,* Part II *(Grotian Papers,* Vol. I), p. 78 *et seq.).*

witnesses and guarantors of the Treaty. The retrospective use made of the gods after decades of warfare between the two rulers suggests that, as in medieval international law,[26] this metaphysical basis of the Treaty was intended to give additional sanctity to the pledged word and reinforce the sanctions system of the Treaty by further, and cumulative, sanctions. Yet, as with other treaties of a similar type—the Eternal Peace Treaties of 532 and 562 between the Byzantine Empire and Persia[27]—these treaties were likely to last little longer than the underlying power equilibrium between the parties involved.

In any case, the draftsmen relied on the safest working principle available in consensual relations: the principle of reciprocity.[28] It must suffice to illustrate the technique employed by reference to the mutual renunciation of aggression between the Contracting Parties: "Rea-mashesha mai Amana, the great king, the king of the land of Egypt, shall not trespass into the Hatti land to take anything therefrom in the future. And Hattušiliš, the great king, the king of the Hatti land, shall not trespass into the land of Egypt to take anything therefrom in the future."

(h) *Rules of international customary law assumed*

To make the *jus aequum* model operative, at least two rules beyond those postulated by the first two models must be assumed:

(1) The Contracting Parties regard their consensual obligations as legally binding.

(2) They accept that any breach of a treaty involves the duty to make reparation.

The general impression left by the treaty material of the period is that contracting parties accepted the existence of such rules. Perhaps this was so because they were familiar with them from their own civil contracts and

26 See, further, *loc. cit.* above, note 17, pp. 128-129.
On the functions of oaths as reinforcements and sanctions of obligations undertaken in ancient international law, see also S. Rosenne, "The Influence of Judaism on the Development of International Law," *6 Netherlands International Law Review* (1958), pp. 141-142.

27 See, further, K. Gueterbock, *Byzanz und Persien* (1906), p. 36 *et seq.*, and S. Verosta, *Die ostroemisch-persischen Vertraege von 562 n. Chr., Anzeiger der phil.-historischen Klasse der Wissenschaften* (1965), No. 10, p. 153 *et seq.*
See also the Treaty of Eternal Peace and Friendship of January 24, 1501, between King Henry VII of England and King James IV of Scotland, *Rymer's Foedera,* Vol. XII, p. 793.

28 For persuasive legal constructions of these obligations, see Korošec, *loc. cit.* above, note 10, pp. 23-25.
On resemblances in the Treaty to legal contracts of the time, see Langdon and Gardiner, *loc. cit.* above, note 11, p. 200.

other forms of consensus, committed to writing under oath or before witnesses.[29]

As is proved by other treaties of the second millennium B.C., the Hittite draftsmen even groped towards rules on good faith in a treaty nexus. They referred to specific hypothetical situations such as those in which fugitives were not directed to the King of Hatti but misdirected, or prisoners who were to be handed over to the King of Hatti but were allowed to escape, and they equated any literal interpretations of such consensual duties with breaches of the oath and, thus, of the treaty obligations of the vassals concerned.[30]

Clauses of this type are lacking in the Treaty of Eternal Peace. The reason may well be that, in comprehensive relations of good brotherhood and good peace between friendly rulers under the aegis of their gods working in the same direction, more was taken for granted than merely the absence of bad faith.

Two clauses in the Treaty in particular appear to bear out the appropriateness of interpreting the Treaty in terms of *jus aequum*.

If interpreted literally, the clause on assistance against external enemies would create an absolute obligation. It would call for unconditional help with the whole armed forces of the party requested, irrespective of any other external or internal commitments.[31] If rulers as shrewd as the Egyptian and Hittite kings attached any legal significance at all to those treaty obligations, they must have known that, with the best will in the world, they could grant and rely on assistance from each other only within the limits of what the requested party considered compatible with its own external and internal security. Moreover, the greater part of the armed forces of both countries had to be raised by levy, and this could be done only when no essential work on the land had to be done. In other words, the obligation had to be equitably interpreted.

The other clauses which suggest that the relationship between the parties itself created equitable relations between the Contracting Parties are the immunity clauses discussed above.[32] The duties of non-punishment enumerated in these clauses are firmly derived from the state of brotherhood existing between the Contracting Parties: They are "verily, brothers; hence ...."

(4) *Oceanic Model*

The Hittite-Egyptian Treaty of Eternal Peace and Brotherhood,

[29] See, further, *ibid.* pp. 50-51, and above, notes 10 and 12-14.
I am greatly obliged to Professor H. S. Smith for the hypothesis, embodied in the last half-sentence.

[30] See, for instance, the Treaty between Mursilis II and Duppi-Tesup, *loc. cit.* above, note 24, p. 19.

[31] See above under (f) (iii).

[32] See above under (f) (v).

concluded more than three thousand years ago, has a chastening topicality: consensual engagements for eternal peace and brotherhood, respect for territorial integrity, renunciation of aggression, a defensive alliance, assistance against threats to internal security and extradition of fugitives.

The Hittite Empire and Egypt, having a joint land frontier with each other and the Hittite Empire being essentially a land Power, little need existed for any stipulations which were based on assumed rules regarding freedom of maritime communications. That such rules were not necessarily lacking is illustrated by a communication of about 1370 B.C. from the King of Alashia (probably Cyprus) to the King of Egypt, complaining of the retention in an Egyptian port of an Alashian ship and Alashian emissaries and merchants.[33] Yet evidence of legal rules on the high seas, comparable in significance to those of European international law during and since the Middle Ages is lacking.

Similarly, it would be unjustified to read into the clauses on the limitation to defensive purposes of the alliance between Hatti and Egypt any view that either party would have considered an offensive alliance against third parties as being illegal.

The history of the Hittite and Egyptian empires and the treaties between the Hittite kings and their vassals[34] would belie any such interpretation. All the references to the defensive character of the alliance meant was that, in the eventuality of an offensive war, the party involved in such a war acted at its own risk. Nevertheless, the Egyptian and Hittite kings were fully alive to the tactical advantages of acting or being thought to act in self-defence.[35]

As mentioned above, it would be more in keeping with the pattern of the early history of international law in comparable systems of international law[36] to assume a different historical premise of the East Mediterranean system of international law in the thirteenth century B.C.: in the absence of agreed states of truce and peace, the normal state of relations between independent entities is war.

33 Exhibit No. 7 in the Paris Exhibition of *Toutankhamon et son temps* (1967). This is probably identical with Letter No. 7 from the King of Alashia to the King of Egypt in J. A. Knudtzon, *Die El-Amarna Tafeln* (1915), pp. 295-297. See also Korošec, *loc. cit.* above, note 14, p. 397.

On the status of the King of Alashia in the fifteenth century B.C. as an independent ruler and "brother" of the King of Egypt, see Knudtzon, *loc. cit.* above, p. 25 *et seq.*, and, on maritime communications between Hatti and Egypt, S. Smith, "Kizzuwadna and Kode," 8 *Journal of Egyptian Archaeology* (1922), p. 46.

34 See below under (5).

On the international relations of the period, see above under (3) and, further, S. Smith, "Kizzuwadna," 10 *Journal of Egyptian Archaeology* (1924), pp. 113—114.

35 The Treaty between King Mursilis II of Hatti and Targasnallis of Hapalla (1352 B.C.?) contains an intriguing evaluation of mankind by the preponderant Party to the Treaty: "Mankind is corrupted." Thus, Targasnallis should not listen to malicious rumours about the King of Hatti (Friedrich, *loc. cit.* above, note 18 (1926), p. 51, note 1), and Korošec, *loc. cit.* above, note 10, p. 76.

See also Korošec, *ibid.* p. 43, on the usefulness of appearing to be a clement ruler.

36 See *loc. cit.* above, note 17, p. 59 *et seq.*

In any case, in the Treaty of Eternal Peace between Egypt and Hatti land the problem of the distinction between self-defence and aggression is solved with a classic elegance on which subsequent ages have found it difficult to improve. For purposes of determining *casus foederis*, self-defence is what my good brother says it is.

Thus, this Treaty foreshadows a model of international law that comes remarkably close to that of pre-1914 international customary law. Barring rules on the freedom of the seas and self-defence, the essential rules underlying five of the fundamental principles of international law are necessarily assumed, however rudimentary or inarticulate some of these rules may have remained: the rules on sovereignty, recognition, responsibility, consent and good faith (in its positive meaning of fair and reasonable dealings). Even in contemporary international law, the limitation of lawful resort to force to action in self-defence is a relatively recent innovation.

(5) *Unionist Model*

The unionist model exists in four major variants: the hegemonial, confederate, federal and unitary sub-models.

In view of the unlimited potentialities of some of these sub-models to change antagonistic types of international society into community relations in the sociological meaning of the term, the unionist model deserves to be treated as a model of its own. In Hegel's terminology, at this point quantity changes into quality, and models of international law become models of potential international order, as distinct from mere quasi-orders.

(a) *The hegemonial sub-model*

The hegemonial sub-model distinguishes itself from the consensual model on a basis of sovereign equality[37] by its emphasis on the hierarchical relations between the parties.

The sub-model may be illustrated by the vassal treaties of the Ḣittite and Assyrian rulers,[38] the hegemonial alignments between Greek city States,[39] the Roman *foedus iniquum*[40] or the Anglo-Scots Treaty of 1174.[41]

37 See above under (3).

38 See, further, Weidner, *loc. cit.* above, note 12, p. 2 *et seq.;* Friedrich, *loc. cit.* above, note 18 (1926), p. 1 *et seq.,* and (1930), p. 42 *et seq.,* and Korošec, *loc. cit.* above, note 10, pp. 72 *et seq.* and 107, and above, note 14, p. 394, and Pritchard, *loc. cit.* above, note 12, pp. 203 and 531 *et seq.*

39 See, for instance, H. Triepel, *Die Hegemonie* (1938—reprinted 1961), p. 362 *et seq.,* and G. Ténékidès, *La notion juridique d'indépendance et la tradition hellénique* (1954).

40 See, for instance, the alliance between Rome and Latium (358 B.C.), Bengtson (ed.), *loc. cit.* above, note 4, No. 302, and Triepel, *loc. cit.* above, note 39, p. 477 *et seq.*

41 See above, note 9.

Whether such relations should be classified as pertaining to the realm of international, national or quasi-international law depends on the circumstances of each individual treaty, especially the intentions of the Contracting Parties.

In the sublimated forms of hegemonial relations in which formal equality of status is squared with the reality of inequality of power, this sub-model has remained of perennial relevance in organised as much as in unorganised international societies.

(b) *The confederate sub-model*

The confederate sub-model is a consensual form of union. In this type of union the sovereignty of all or some of its members remains substantially intact. Without express consent or acquiescence by member States, the confederate organs may communicate authoritatively only with the governments of their member States but have no direct access to their citizens.

The pattern has been tried extensively in ancient China[42] of the seventh century B.C., the Iroquois Confederacy of the Five (and subsequently Six) Nations of 1675,[43] the declining days of the Holy Roman Empire of the German Nation[44] and the Germanic Confederation of 1815.[45] In the League of Nations and the United Nations, it has been revived on a universalist basis as a quasi-constitutional framework of the organised post-1919 and post-1945 international societies.[46]

42 The first of these unions—formally all of them within the feudal framework of the Chinese Empire of their times—lasted from 679 to 643 B.C.
See, further, for instance, R. L. Walker, *The Multi-State System of Ancient China* (1953).

43 On the "Great Law" and "Great Peace" of this Union, known as the "Long-house," the "Completed Cabin" and the "United Nations," see C. Colden, *The History of the Five Indian Nations* (1866); P. A. W. Wallace, *Pennsylvania. Seed of a Nation* (1962), p. 25 *et seq.;* D. E. Leach, *The Northern Colonial Frontier 1607—1763* (1966), p. 11; on the subsequent Indian Confederation, planned between 1790 and 1794 by the Six Nations for thirty-five nations, R. C. Downes, *Council Fires on the Upper Ohio* (1940), pp. 282 *et seq.* and 299, and, on the history since 1860 of the loyalist Iroquois settled in Canada, J. A. Noon, *Law and Government of the Grand River Iroquois* (1949), p. 45 *et seq.* See also 11 *London Quarterly of World Affairs* (1945), p. 217; R. Numelin, *The Beginnings of Diplomacy* (1950), p. 244 *et seq.*, and L. C. Green, "Canada's Indians," 4 Ottawa L.R. (1970), p. 101 *et seq.*

44 S. Pufendorf, *Gruendlicher Bericht von dem Zustande des H. Reichs Teutscher Nation* and *Untersuchung von der Beschaffenheit eines irregulairen Staates* (1667—Leipzig ed., 1715); the realistic account of what Pufendorf had termed *"ein ungestaltes Wesen" (irregulare aliquod monstro simile*—Chap VI, para 9—*ibid.* p. 696) in No. 19 (A. Hamilton and J. Madison) of *The Federalist* (1787-8) and, for a perceptive recent treatment, A. Randelzhofer, *Voelkerrechtliche Aspekte des Heiligen Roemischen Reiches nach 1648* (1967).

45 For the text of the *deutsche Bundesakte* of June 8, 1815, see A. Michaelis, *Corpus Juris Publici Germanici* (1825), p. 450 *et seq.*, or E. Hertslet, *The Map of Europe by Treaty,* Vol. I (1875), p. 200 *et seq.*, and, further, L. v. Dresch, *Oeffentliches Recht des deutschen Bundes* (1820), p. 37 *et seq.*

46 See, further, *loc. cit.* above, note 17, p. 18 *et seq.*

(c) *The federal sub-model*

This model has two variants of its own, those of political and functional federation. While the former is illustrated by the establishment of the German Reich in 1870-71 on a consensual basis, the latter is exemplified by the supranational experiments of the three European Communities.

(d) *The unitary sub-model*

If independent States desire to take this line, they also are free to transform themselves into a unitary State on a consensual basis. *Deditio*, as practised by the Roman Republic,[47] and the union between England and Wales with Scotland of 1707[48] invite reflection on the elasticity of the consensual model. In its extreme and universal application, it brings us back to our starting point in the shape of the universal and unitary State.[49]

III—TOWARDS A COMPARATIVE HISTORY OF INTERNATIONAL LAW

In an earlier Section of this Chapter, the paradox of the remarkable continuity in the rules of international law, as distinct from the discontinuities in its overriding *de facto* quasi-orders, has been explained by reference to recurring needs in post-war periods of contemporary international society and other comparable international societies for similar rules of international customary law. They have been characterised as essentially formal, jurisdictional, enabling and lubricating rules which, in the absence of further consensual obligations, are left to auto-interpretation by all concerned.

47 See, for instance, the Treaty on the Campanian *deditio* of 343 B.C., Bengtson (ed.), *loc. cit.* above, note 4, No. 335, and that of 378 B.C. concerning Latium and Capua, *ibid.*, No. 347, and further, Heuss, *loc. cit.* above, note 4, p. 60 *et seq.*

48 Treaty on Articles of Union, July 22, 1706; Act of Union, March 6, 1707 (6 Anne, cap. 11); Union operative since May 1, 1707.

For an instructive account of the negotiations and parliamentary discussions in Edinburgh and London, which preceded the Union and anticipated most of the arguments for and against British membership of the European Communities, see T. Smollet, *The History of England from the Revolution in 1688,* Vol. II (1810), pp. 165 *et seq.*, 203 *et seq.*, and 229 *et seq.*, and, for an attempt made in 1713 to dissolve the Union, *ibid.* p. 463 *et seq.*

Queen Anne's Order in Council of July 23, 1706, has also some topical interest: Whoever should be concerned in any discourse or libel or in laying wagers relating to the Union, should be prosecuted with the utmost rigour of the law *(ibid.* p. 205).

See, further, *The Acts of the Parliament of Scotland,* Vol. XI: *1702—1707* (1824); W. L. Mathieson, *Scotland and the Union, 1695-1745* (2 vols.—1905); C. S. Terry, The Scottish Parliament. Its Constitution and Procedure 1603-1707 (1905); Th. Keith, *Commercial Relations of England and Scotland 1603-7* (1910); P. Hume Brown, *The Legislative Union of England and Scotland* (1914); A. V. Dicey and R. S. Rait, *Thoughts on the Union between England and Scotland* (1920); G. S. Pryde (ed.), *The Treaty of Union of Scotland and England 1707* (1950); T. C. Smout, "The Road to Union" in G. K. Holmes (ed.), *Britain after the Glorious Revolution, 1689-1714* (1969), p. 176 *et seq.;* W. Ferguson, "The Making of the Treaty of Union of 1707," 43 *Scottish Historical Review* (1964), p. 89 *et seq.*, and T. C. Smout and R. H. Campbell, 'The Anglo-Scottish Union of 1707," 16 (2nd ser.) *Economic History Review* (1964), p. 455 *et seq.*

49 See above under I.

Yet, this answer poses a further problem. Why, in a history of international relations which extends over millennia, should these models, so similar and so limited, have so much recommended themselves? Beyond this, why is it that even in a world society such as our own, with an abundance of international institutions, the picture has changed so little, as compared with the international society of Hattušiliš III and Ramesses II?

The clue lies in the similarity of the political infra-structures of the international societies, which, since time immemorial, have come and gone. In essence, they were—and are—systems of power politics, open or in disguise. They all employ law to serve subordinate purposes between potential enemies or cement closer relations between potential or actual allies or States in transition to a functional or territorial federation. Yet they fall short of verifiable commitments which, more than nominally or without extensive contracting-out clauses, limit the super-Powers of their age.

Thus, the history of international law confirms and supplements the findings of a sociological interpretation of contemporary international law.

The combined results of these inter-disciplinary tests are that, in an international society as distinct from a community, the models of international law adopted by State practice are repetitive rather than continuous in their legal validity. They are adopted again and again because they correspond to stereotyped needs of societies which are motivated by the quest for power rather than law and based on the co-existence of entities which consider themselves as ends rather than means.

Even on this society footing, the Treaty of Kadesh shows the way to reasonably stable relations between sovereign States in the category of greater Powers: substantive reciprocity of legal rights and duties.

If States desire to go beyond the security which a law of reciprocity can give them and transform their society relations into community relations in the strict sociological meaning of the term, the Treaty of Kadesh points the way to the spirit in which such more exacting duties must be visualised and fulfilled: We are "verily brothers, hence....."

It remains to summarise the specific characteristics of the models approach to the history of international law:

To achieve the highest efficiency of the models approach, which serves to present a comprehensive and accurate if simplified picture of the historical reality of international law, it requires a wide inter-disciplinary treatment of the history of international law. It should be based on the findings of comparative history, sociology and anthropology on the rise, fall and overlapping of civilisations and awareness of the sequence of, frequently parallel or interlocking, systems of international relations.

The models approach should be based on a clear distinction for any particular period under discussion between the actual rules of international law and those of its correlated international quasi-order.

While the models approach is compatible with any other treatment of international law in historical perspective,[50] it may claim seven distinct features of its own:

(1) It dispenses with fictitious genealogies of contemporary international law. Conversely, it assists in a detached reassessment of any claims made at any time to the rise of a "new" or "modern" international law.

(2) It allows for the more adequate treatment—and not merely as precursors of the one and only international law—of defunct or arrested systems of international law.

(3) It avoids unnecessary forms of geographical or ethnical "centrism" and parochialism regarding the special connection between international law as such with any particular part of the world and permits due account being taken of comparable illustrations chosen from different epochs and continents.

(4) By emphasis on the need for the distinction, at any particular time, between the rules of international customary law and their consensual superstructures, it contributes to a better understanding of the character of the rules of international customary law and these superstructures.

(5) While, within each model, the applicable rules can receive proper attention, the comparative treatment of the material should assist in avoiding unnecessary multiplication of such material and reduce a great deal of it to illustrations of more or less significant variations of the major models.

(6) The models approach allows for the emphasis to be shifted from secondary to primary material.

(7) Any claim for the addition to existing historical models of international law—or deletion from their number—can be decided by examination whether such a model calls its own a distinct system of rules of international law. It is by reference to this test that the need for a new model—and, conversely, its redundancy—is proved.

50 See, further, *loc. cit.* above, note 17 (1962), Chap. 3: "International Law in Historical Perspective," and, for recent illustrations of different techniques in the field of the History of International Law, see, for instance, J.H. Verzijl's monumental study, which, by an auspicious coincidence, bears the same title (1968-1975); C. H. Alexandrowicz, *An Introduction to the History of the Law of Nations in the East Indies* (16th, 17th and 18th centuries—1967), and the *Grotian Society Papers,* Vol. I (loc. cit. above, note 25) and Vol. II (1968—Nijhoff, The Hague).

Chapter 4

EQUITY IN INTERNATIONAL LAW

> "When passions have been so excited on both sides that no common standard of justice can be found, and what one party insists on as a right the other denounces as a wrong, prejudice may become too headstrong to yield to the voice of equity" (Ch. Bankhead, British Chargé d'Affaires, to J. Forsyth, Secretary of State, Washington, January 27, 1836—24 *British and Foreign State Papers*, p. 1158).
>
> "As I understand, the skull of the sufferer is injured, and he is not in opulent circumstances, a pecuniary compensation is both an equitable and a legal demand on his part" (Lord Malmesbury to Lord Westmoreland (Vienna), Foreign Office, April 28, 1852—42 *ibid.* p. 516).

The scope of the issue becomes manifest from reflection on the number of synonyms and facets of equity in international law, let alone other branches of law. At least five come readily to mind: prohibition of the abuse of rights, estoppel, jurisdiction *ex aequo et bono,* laches and prohibition of *venire contra factum proprium.*

Closely related terms such as good neighbourliness and justice, and fields of international law in which equitable considerations have exercised a strong formative influence also call for attention. Rules such as those on acquisitive and extinctive prescription, the minimum standard of civilisation regarding the treatment of foreign nationals, treaty interpretation and the reparation of international torts belong to this category.

Thus, the task is really to analyse the whole of international law from the angle of equity and if possible isolate the equity element in international law.

The equity contents vary from one legal system and one branch of law to another. Moreover, they may expand and shrink in the course of the evolution and decay of any one of these systems and branches of law. These reflections alone counsel against any sweeping generalisation of a speculative, deductive or eclectic character. In any case, such generalising assertions are likely to be unverifiable by hard evidence. To this extent, they are acceptable but as expressions of faith, hope and indoctrination.[1]

[1] For fuller bibliographies, see the writer's *International Law as Applied by International Courts and Tribunals,* Vol. 1: *General Principles* (1957) (subsequently abbreviated as *Vol. I*), pp. 703-705; Vol III: *International Constitutional Law (1976) (subsequently abbreviated as Vol.III)*, p. 644 *et seq.*, and the "Reports on Legal Aspects of World Affairs" under the heading of "Foundations" in the *Year Book of World Affairs,* Vols 11 (1957)-25 (1971).

A few distinct contributions may be singled out: G. Radbruch, "Justice and Equity in International Relations" in N. Benwich and Others, *Justice and Equity in the International Sphere* (1936), p. 1 *et seq.*: M. Sørensen, *Les Sources du droit international* (1946), p. 191 *et*

Continued on next Page

In these circumstances, it is advisable to take little for granted and explain the techniques employed in this Chapter more fully than would otherwise be necessary.

On the basis of earlier studies, three working hypotheses suggest themselves:

(1) The rules of most developed legal systems can be divided into rules of *jus strictum* and *jus aequum*. Rights of *jus strictum* are absolute and may be exercised irrespective of equitable considerations. Rights of *jus aequum* are relative and must be exercised reasonably and in good faith.

(2) The movement from primitive and archaic legal systems to mature and developed legal systems tends to be accompanied by a change in emphasis from *jus strictum* to *jus aequum*.

(3) *Jus aequum* or equity means the infusion of considerations of reasonableness and good faith into legal relations. The rule postulating the application of these standards may be termed the *jus aequum* rule.

To test as objectively as possible these working hypotheses and the significance of the *jus aequum* rule in international law, it is proposed to examine the problem from three angles:

to view it in historical perspective;

to deal separately, and on various levels of international integration, with asserted rules;

to rely, whenever possible, on evidence of the highest persuasive value, that is, international judicial authority. It is, however, necessary to be aware of potential failings even in what, otherwise, may well be considered to be the best evidence available: owing to the consensual basis of all international arbitration and adjudication, this law-determining agency tends to overstate the equity contents of rules of international customary law. International judicial organs may be expressly authorised to rely on general principles of law or may take it upon themselves to exercise this authority. References to equity or its synonyms may be contained merely in judicial *obiter dicta* or reservations, intended to safeguard the freedom of international judicial organs, but do not necessarily form part of the operative parts of decisions. They can hardly be adduced as authorities on international equity.[2]

2 For illustrations, see loc. cit. above note 1, *Vol. 1*, pp. 47-48, 51-54 and 175-176.

Continued from previous Page

seq.; A. Verdross, *Die bona fides als Grundlage des Voelkerrechts (Laun-Festschrift*—1953), p. 29 *et seq.;* Bin Cheng, *General Principles of Law as Applied by International Courts and Tribunals* (1953), pp. 48 and 400 *et seq.; and "Justice and Equity in International Law," 8 C.L.P. (1955), p. 185 et seq.,* C.W. Jenks, *The Prospects of International Adjudication* (1964), p. 316 *et seq.;* Ch. Rousseau, *Droit International Public,* Vol. 1 (1970), p. 393 *et seq.;* V. Degan *L'équité et le droit international* (1970); and J.P. Mueller, *Vertrauensschutz im Voelkerrecht* (1971).

I—INTERNATIONAL EQUITY IN HISTORICAL PERSPECTIVE

To view equity in operation from the historical angle is likely to be helpful in several ways:

It is simpler to find one's bearings in the more straightforward environments of the systems of open power politics of the past than in the more sophisticated environments of contemporary world society.

With the assistance of historical models which provide inbuilt safeguards against comparing the incomparable,[3] it is possible to analyse in a verifiable form the impact of equity as a formative factor in the shaping of international law and thus avoid an unduly static treatment of the subject.

Against the background of experiments stretching over almost four millennia, it is easier to assess with detachment and a sense of humour current fashions and exuberances in this as in other fields of international law.

Within the limits of this paper, two case studies from the second millennium B.C. and medieval international law must suffice.

(a) *Hittite State practice*

The first of these case studies is drawn from Hittite State practice in the fourteenth and thirteenth centuries B.C. It becomes apparent from the treaties concluded between Hittite rulers and foreign sovereigns as well as with semi-independent vassals that the draftsmen of these treaties attempted to cope with a difficult problem.

They intended to limit by written commitments the freedom of action of the contracting parties, yet they realised the risk of misconstruction of words in bad faith. Thus, by concrete illustrations, they tried to anticipate typical evasions and circumventions by contracting parties of their treaty obligations.

A few illustrations will drive home the point. In a treaty between a Hittite King and Lab'u (possibly the mayor of Tunip) and the inhabitants of Tunip (1394 B.C.?), the latter undertakes to hand over prisoners of war to Hatti. Yet, if anybody hides a prisoner, he "will be like one who does not take a prisoner."[4]

In other treaties, acts of treachery in general and acts specified as such are singled out. For instance, omission to keep watch against the enemy or unwillingness to fight "in the refusal of his heart" are singled out as breaches of the oath, which makes the treaty binding and, therefore, as

3 See, further, above, Chapter 3.

4 E.F. Weidner, *Politische Dokumente aus Kleinasien (Boghaskoei-Studien,* ed by O. Weber, Hefte 8 and 9 (1923)—reprint 1970).

For illustrations of deceit and craftiness (*astute interpretari,* as Zwinger put it) in the interpretation of treaties in ancient and more recent times, see Th. Zwinger, *Theatrum Vitae Humanae* (1565); Bodin's *Six livres de la république* (1576), Bk V, Chap. VI, and A. Gentili, *De Jure Belli Libri Tres* (1612), Bk. II Chap IV. See also L. W. Beilenson, *The Treaty Trap* (1969).

breaches of the treaty.[5] Similarly, the use of witchcraft by one party against the other is expressly prohibited.[6]

The treaty between Mursilis II of Hatti and Duppi-Tesup of Amarra is especially instructive. If the vassal is asked to do something that had been agreed, he is either to say at once that he cannot do it or he must carry out his obligation. Otherwise, he breaks his oath.[7] Similarly, if Duppi-Tesup does not direct foreign fugitives to the Great King of Hatti but misdirects them into the wilderness or fails to arrest an escaped prisoner of the Hittites, he is in breach of his oath.

As in other archaic systems of law,[8] bad faith is no defence against the fulfilment of obligations of *jus strictum*. It is for the parties concerned to protect themselves as best they can against dishonest or sharp practices.

This was exactly what the draftsmen of the Hittite treaties tried to do when they specified acts of bad faith incompatible with the oath and treaty obligations of the contracting parties concerned. In doing so, they elaborated implicitly the standards of good faith expected from the parties to their treaties. On this consensual basis, good faith, as contrasted with bad faith, became incorporated in the international law of the east Mediterranean inter-State system of the second millennium B.C.[9]

Another treaty, probably concluded between 1325 and 1305 B.C., marks the transition from good faith, excluding merely bad faith, to good faith as a facet of *jus aequum*. In this treaty, the staleness of a claim is given as the reason for not insisting on it.[10]

(b) *Early English State practice*

In a system of international relations in western Europe that is comparable to the east Mediterranean inter-State system of the late second

5 Treaty between Subbiluliuma, King of Hatti, and Tette, King of Nuhassi (Weidner p. 61).

6 Treaty between Mutwatalli, King of Hatti, and Sunassura, King of Kizwatna (*ibid.* p. 103).

7 J. Friedrich, *Staatsvertraege des Hatti Reiches in hethitischer Sprache,* Part I (31 *Mitteilungen der Vorderasiatisch-Aegyptischen Gessellschaft* (1926.1), pp. 19-21).

8 For an illustration of the binding character of an oath and the peace and league made under it in spite of the oath having been obtained by deceit, see the *Old Testament,* Joshua, Chap. 9.

On the infusion of *jus aequum* into *jus strictum* in archaic systems of law, see, for instance, Henry Sumner Maine, *Ancient Law* (1861), Chaps. III and IX; J.B. Ames, *Lectures on Legal History* (1913), p. 435 *et seq.;* Paul Vinogradoff, *Outlines of Historical Jurisprudence,* Vol. 1 (1920), p. 344 *et seq.;* Frederick Pollock and Frederick William Maitland, *The History of English Law,* Vol. II (1923), p. 184 *et seq.;* W. Friedmann, *The Contribution of English Equity to the Ideal of an International Equity Tribunal* (1935); W.W. Buckland and A.D. McNair, *Roman Law and Common Law* (1936), Chap. XI (4-5); F. Schulz, *Principles of Roman Law* (1936), Chap. XI; H.F. Jolowicz, *Historical Introduction to the Study of Roman Law* (1936), Chap. XVII (II); W. Seagle, *The Quest for Law* (1941), Bks. II -IV; A.D.S. Diamond, *Primitive Law* (1950), pp. 348-349; and Th. Plucknett, *A Concise History of the Common Law* (1956), p. 677 *et seq.*

9 See, further, Chapter 3 above, section III.

On the clause "*conservato sine dolo malo*" in *foedera iniqua* between the Roman Republic and her allies, see, for instance, H. Triepel, *Die Hegemonie* (1939—reprinted 1961), p. 477.

10 Treaty between Mutwatalli, King of Hatti, and Alaksandus, King of Wilusa, *loc. cit.* above, note 7, Part II (*ibid.* 34 (1930), pp. 51-52).

millennium B.C.,[11] good faith, as opposed to bad faith, made its way into early English treaty practice.

From this point of view, the Anglo-Scots Treaty of A.D. 1174 is instructive. By this treaty, King William of Scotland, then a prisoner in English hands, became the vassal of King Henry II of England.

Throughout the treaty, good faith is contrasted with bad faith. The fact that William of Scotland acted under coercion was not considered to impair the good faith of King Henry II nor the validity of King William's obligations.[12] This view of the matter was confirmed by the Bull of Pope Gregory IX of January 4, 1235, in which the treaty of 1174 was described as an agreement "freely accepted" by Scotland.[13]

In subsequent practice, fraud was equated with malice. It was stipulated that treaties were to be observed, applied and interpreted in good faith, without malice, fraudulent intent or circumvention (*absque omni dolo et fraude* or *absque ulla fictione).*[14]

At this point, the transition was made, at least for purposes of treaty law, from *jus strictum* to *jus aequum* in the evolution of European international law.

(c) *Two further working hypotheses*

In the present state of the inductive and comparative study of the History of International Law, it would be premature to generalise unduly from isolated case studies such as those summarised under the two previous headings.

Yet, these practices, remote as they are from each other in time but comparable in their wider settings, appear to lend support to at least two further working hypotheses:[15]

(4) In rudimentary systems of international law, good faith tends to

11 See, further, the writer's *The Frontiers of International Law* (1962), p. 85 *et seq.*

12 See. E.L.G. Stones (ed.), *Anglo-Scottish Relations 1174-1328* (1965), p. 2 *et seq.*, and *Rymer's Foedera,* Vol. 1, p. 40.

13 Stones, *loc. cit.* above, note, 12, p. 37.
See also *loc. cit.* above, Chapter 3, under II (2) and (3)

14 See, for instance, Art. 6 of the Convention of Subsidy of May 17, 1101 (1110) between King Henry I of England and King Robert of Flanders, *Rymer's Foedera,* Vol. I, p. 1 (for the date, see also C. Parry and Ch. Hopkins (eds.), *Index of British Treaties 1101-1968* (1970), Vol. 2 p. 3): "*Quae praedictae summonitiones propter hoc inventae non sint, sine malo ingenio.*" Art. 6 of the Treaty of Subsidy of March 10, 1103 (1101) between the same (*Rymer's Foedera,* Vol 1, *ibid.* p. 4); the Treaty of March 19, 1163, between King Henry II of England and his son Henry, on the one hand, and Count Theodore of Flanders: "*Juvabunt eos per bonam fidem*" (Art. 9—*ibid.* p. 23), "*quod nulla praedictarum summonitionum inventa sit, per dolum, vel per malum ingenium*" (Art. 10—*ibid.* p. 24) and "*per bonam fidem, absque omni dolo et malo ingenio*" (Art. 39—*ibid.* p. 26) and a letter from King Henry II of May 14, 1321, to the Pope, in which named emissaries are described as true Israelites "*in quibus dolus non est*" (*ibid.* Vol. III, p. 884).

15 See above, Introductory Section.

fulfil primarily its minimal functions of excluding bad faith and the evasion of legal obligations.

(5)In closer consensual relations, good faith tends to lose this essentially negative quality of absence of bad faith. It acquires positive characteristics which approximate it to *jus aequùm* in the positive meaning of the term.

It is in the light of the five working hypotheses and the tests elaborated so far that the place and functions of equity in contemporary international law will have to be analysed.

II—EQUITY AND THE LAW-CREATING PROCESSES OF INTERNATIONAL LAW

In answering the question how far equity has permeated the province of international law, the first task is to establish whether the *jus aequum* rule has been incorporated into any one or more of the three primary law-creating processes of international law: treaties, international customary law and the general principles of law recognised by civilised nations.

(a) *Treaties*

More than any other law-creating process, treaties remain the least controversial form in which to translate normative but non-legal precepts, such as those of any particular brand of natural law or international morality, into rules of general or particular international law.

On a near-universal level, this task has been performed in the Charter of the United Nations and the Statute of the International Court of Justice. In accordance with Paragraph 2 of Article 2 of the Charter, "all members, in order to ensure to all of them the rights and benefits resulting from membership, shall fulfil in good faith the obligations assumed by them in accordance with the present Charter."

In addition to other clauses supporting the reception of the principle of good neighbourliness in the Charter of the United Nations, it is prescribed in Article 74 of the Charter of the United Nations that the policies of members must be based in relation to non-self-governing territories, "no less than in respect of their metropolitan areas," on the "general principle of good neighbourliness."

The general principles of law recognised by civilised nations are expressly included in Article 38 of the Statute of the International Court of Justice. For practical purposes, this has made the question largely hypothetical whether, in the absence of such a provision, these general principles of law constitute one of the law-creating processes of international law. Thus, to any extent to which comparative lawyers are able to furnish evidence that justice, equity and other moral values are recognised in the world's major legal systems as general principles of law, this clause serves as a vehicle of general reception of equity into international law within the orbit of the International Court of Justice.

In numerous arbitration treaties, parties have incorporated equity clauses supplementing the *jus strictum* of international customary law. These clauses clarify unequivocally that the parties desire the tribunal to which they submit their case to apply international law in the spirit of *jus aequum.*[16]

If parties to cases before the International Court of Justice so desire, they are authorised by Article 38 of the Court's Statute to empower the Court to decide a case between them *ex aequo et bono*. In this eventuality, the Court may dispense equity so as to override actual rules of international law.[17]

(b) *International customary law*

In determining the equity content of specific rules of international customary law, it is essential to remember how many of these rules are the product of centuries of treaty experiments. They range from the rules regarding the protection of foreign nationals and ships in distress to those on the application and interpretation of treaties and international responsibility.[18]

These rules became embodied in international customary law whenever, in relation to any one of these rules, it could be taken for granted that, in the view of individual contracting parties, they had become generally accepted as law.

At this point, States which had formerly repeated such clauses in treaty after treaty ceased to do so in their relations with States with which they shared a common ethical denominator. Especially this was true between western States. Significantly, however, such States continued to insert some of these clauses in treaties with new States which could not be

16 Thus, in Art. 25 of the Treaty of Peace and Alliance of July 10, 1654, between Cromwell and King Jean IV of Portugal, the settlement of outstanding claims *"ex jure et aequo"* is provided (J. Dumont, *Corps universel diplomatique,* Vol. 6, Part II, p. 85).

See, also, below under (c) and, further K. Strupp, "Le droit du juge international de statuer selon l'équité," Hague Academy of International Law, *Recueil,* Vol. 33 (1930), p. 351 *et seq.;* G. Berlia, *Essai sur la portée de la clause de jugement en équité en droit des gens* (1937); R.R. Wilson, "The Jurisprudence of National Claims Commissions." 36 A.J.I.L. (1942), p. 65 *et seq.;* and K.S. Carlston, *The Process of International Arbitration* (1946). p. 155 *et seq.;*

17 See, further, M. Habicht, *The Power of the International Judge to give a décision ex aequo et bono* (1935), and Arts. 29-30 of the Protocol of the Commission of Mediation, Conciliation and Arbitration of the Organisation of African Unity, July 21, 1964, 3 *International Legal Materials* (1964), p. 1123.

For judgments which, on grounds of the duty of the Court to do justice, the inherently equitable character of relevant rules and admissions of the parties, tend towards *ex aequo et bono* decisions, see the *North Sea Continental Shelf Cases (I.C.J. Reports 1969,* pp. 47 and 88), and the *Icelandic Fisheries Jurisdiction Cases* (*ibid.* , 1974, pp. 31-33); Judge Koretsky (Diss. Op.), *ibid.1969*, pp. 165-167; Judge Tanaka (Diss. Op.), *ibid.*, p. 196; Judge Morelli (Diss. Op.), *ibid.*, pp. 207 and 213-214, and Judge Gros (Diss. Op.), *ibid., 1974,* pp. 143 and 146-149. See also E.D. Brown, *The Legal Regime of Hydrospace* (1971), p. 41 *et seq.*

18 See further above, Introd. Section, and below under III (a).

expected to be fully aware of, or observe, these rules or in treaties with States on the fringes of western civilisation.

The time when these clauses were dropped, limited in use or relegated to more subordinate places such as instruments of ratification, as with the good-faith clause on the interpretation and application of treaties,[19] makes it possible to trace with relative accuracy the transition of a rule of international law with strong equitable content from a consensual footing to that of international customary law.

(c) *The general principles of law*

It is likely that comparative research will establish a common core of equity in the world's most representative legal systems. Yet, this does not mean that equity is all-prevading in most of these systems, especially if these happen to be the laws of totalitarian or authoritarian States.

Even if this aspect of the matter could be ignored, the question of the place of the general principles of law in the hierarchy of the law-creating processes of international law arises. In actual practice, this question, put in the abstract, is of little importance. In international judicial practice, for instance, the problem does not present itself in this form at all, but as one of competing rules of international law. In other words, it is hierarchies between individual products of the three law-creating processes, and not between the law-creating processes themselves, that have to be settled.

To judge by what international courts and tribunals actually do, they tend to give first priority to treaties and second place to relevant rules of international customary law. In particular, the Permanent Court of International Justice and the International Court of Justice have shown a marked reserve to the application of general principles of law in the operative parts of their judicial pronouncements, as distinct from isolated *obiter dicta* and reservations of judicial discretion.[20]

Thus, leaving aside the incorporation of equity in treaties, the crucial question, which remains to be more fully discussed, is the place of equity in international customary law, that is, in unorganised international society.

19 See, further, Hague Academy of International Law, *Recueil,* Vol. 87 (1955), p. 295 *et seq.*

20 On the auxiliary application of general principles of law recognised by civilised nations, frequently employed synonymously with *jus aequum,* by "conciliation"—actually, arbitration—commissions under the Peace Treaty of 1947 with Italy, see the writer's *International Law as Applied by International Courts and Tribunals,* Vol. II: *The Law of Armed Conflict* (1968) (subsequently abbreviated as *Vol. II),* p. 741, note 35. See also the Nambia case (I.C.J. Reports 1971, p. 47).

See, further, *Vol. I,* p. 54 *et seq.,* and, for significant reflections on the subject, G.I. Tunkin, *Droit international public* (1965), p. 119 *et seq.,* and "General Principles of Law" in International Law" in R. Marcic and Others (eds), *Internationale Festschrift fuer Alfred Verdross* (1971), p. 523 *et seq.*

On the unreliability of legal maxims, which, as a rule, are neutralised by counter-maxims, as substitutes for general principles of law which are duly established by comparative research, see, further, the writer's *The Inductive Approach to International Law* (1965), p. 49 *et. seq.*

III—EQUITY IN THE SYSTEM OF CONTEMPORARY INTERNATIONAL LAW

It is advisable to analyse the problem of equity on various levels of international integration: unorganised international society, partly organised international society, international society organised on the confederate level of the United Nations and its Specialised Agencies, and within supranational associations.

(a) *Equity in unorganised international society*

The chief rules of international customary law can be classified under the heads of seven fundamental principles: sovereignty, recognition, consent, freedom of the seas, international responsibility, self-defence and good faith. Other rules are the result of the interplay between rules governing two or more of these principles.[21]

To avoid over-generalisation, the impact of the *jus aequum* rule on the rules of international law will be examined principle by principle.

(1) *Sovereignty.* The rights of freedom under international law are as much part of international law as the rules governing the other fundamental principles of international customary law which limit this freedom under the law.

Actually, the rules on sovereignty are considerably strengthened by the presumption in favour of the good faith of the subjects of international law. In the absence of convincing evidence to the contrary, this presumption tends to operate towards non-liability of the subjects of international law.

Thus, in the case of *Certain German Interests in Polish Upper Silesia* (1926), the Permanent Court of International Justice held that the conditional abandonment by Germany of her rights and titles under Article 88 of the Peace Treaty of Versailles of 1919 could not involve the immobilisation of all movable and immovable property belonging to the German State during the period from the day of the coming into force of the Peace Treaty until the transfer of sovereignty over Upper Silesia. Germany retained until the actual transfer of sovereignty the right to dispose of her property, and "only a misuse of this right could endow an act of alienation with the character of a breach of the Treaty; such misuse cannot be presumed, and it rests with the party who states that there has been such misuse to prove his statement."[22]

While the Permanent Court of International Justice never actually applied the doctrine of the abuse of rights,[23] the International Court of

21 See, further, below under (8), *Vol. I*, p. 289 *et seq.; Vol II*, p. 673 *et seq.*, and *loc. cit.* above, note 20, *Inductive Approach* (1965), pp. 80 and 95 *et seq.*

22 Series A. No. 7, p. 30.
See also below under (5).

23 See, further, the writer's *International Law and Order* (1971), p. 84 *et seq.*

Justice did so in one case: the *Anglo-Norwegian Fisheries Case* (1951). It applied the concept of abuse of rights in its formulation of the rule governing the base-line of the territorial sea.[24]

Actually, the rule, as formulated by the Court, was so vague that if the Court did not want it to become a justification of uncontrolled licence, it had no choice but to curb it by reservations regarding manifest abuse, moderation and reasonableness, that is, reliance again on the *jus aequum* rule.[25]

The Court explained that in what it considered to be the exceptional circumstances of the case before it, the application of the rule laid down was not to be too closely examined. It sufficed that the base-line of the territorial sea should follow the general direction of the coast and keep *inter fauces terrarum.* Except in the case of "manifest abuse," small-scale charts of the coastlines as a whole would most closely convey the Court's ruling.[26]

If the geographical characteristics of the Norwegian coastline are taken to be less exceptional than the Court assumed,[27] it becomes even clearer how easily, in relation to maritime frontiers, the *jus aequum* rule, as formulated by the International Court of Justice, can be employed to buttress territorial sovereignty and limit the scope of the rules underlying the principle of the freedom of the seas.[28]

It must also be recalled that State practice has refused to apply altogether the *jus aequum* rule in a number of fields in which it has preferred to secure reasonable behaviour by willingness to answer in kind any unreasonable exercise of sovereign discretion. Thus, States are free at any time, and without any explanation, to declare a diplomatic or consular representative *persona non grata.* Yet, if they choose to take this course unreasonably or arbitrarily, they must expect the State adversely affected to retaliate in kind. The result may be similar to the prohibition of an abuse of the right of declaring a foreign representative *persona non grata.* Yet, it is not achieved by relativising absolute rights but by opposing one absolute right to another.[29]

(2) *Recognition.* Subject to respect for the sovereignty of other full subjects of international law—this explains the prohibition of premature recognition—discretionary power reigns supreme in this field. Equity may be dispensed as a matter of discretion or even as an imagined legal duty but neither makes a new law. Even so, equity is not entirely absent

24 *I.C.J. Reports 1951,* p. 142.

25 See also above, note 17, and, further, *Vol. I,* p. 319 *et seq.*

26 *I.C.J. Reports 1951,* p. 142.
See also Judge Sir Arnold McNair's Diss. Op., *ibid.* p. 166 *et seq.,* and Judge Hsu Mo's Sep. Op., pp. 154-155.

27 See Judge Sir Arnold McNair's Diss. Op., *ibid.* pp. 169-170, and Judge Read's Diss. Op., *ibid.* p. 193.

28 See below under (4).

29 See also below under (6) and (b) and, further, *loc. cit* above, note 23, p. 100 *et seq.*

from this field. Within limits varying according to the intent expressed, recognition, once granted, creates an estoppel. This prevents the party obligated from going back on its unilateral act.[30]

(3) *Consent.* In the context of treaties as one of the three primary law-creating processes, illustrations have been offered of the transformation by way of treaty of the whole or part of the *jus aequum* rule into rules of international law. [31]

Similarly, the growth of the equity rule on the interpretation and application of treaties behind the façades of judicial logic is a fascinating instance of equity as a law-shaping factor. The rule, as it has grown, demands reasonableness and good faith in the interpretation and application of treaties. It is the object of this rule to exclude contradiction, arbitrariness and absurdity from the interpretation and application of treaties and to regulate on this footing the conduct of individual contracting parties.[32]

Whether in the form of express consent, acquiescence, tacit assent, or unilateral and complementary acts which create treaty engagements, any of these consensual transactions produces an estoppel. The reason for this is that this view of the interplay of the rules governing consent and good faith corresponds to the typical intent of the parties concerned.[33]

Estoppels produced by consent operate irrespective of the reasonable and reciprocal character of individual consensual engagements. Such undertakings may be unreasonable, one-sided or both. Those involved are free to please themselves, and sovereign States are entitled to their own fair shares of sovereign stupidity.

In such a situation, the two chief branches of the *jus aequum* rule—good faith and reasonableness—part company. The unequivocally declared intention of parties to a treaty may put the reasonableness branch of the *jus aequum* rule out of action. Even so, its good-faith branch remains fully operative and in such a contingency the *jus aequum* rule continues to fulfil an important function. To be effective, consensual *jus strictum* of a one-sided or unreasonable character must be stated in the most explicit terms. Otherwise it is likely to be reinterpreted in terms of *jus aequum* rule.[34]

Under international customary law, neither the *jus aequum* rule nor any other rule of international law constitutes part of *jus cogens.*[35] To give it this character requires a consensual effort. This is what happened, for instance, in the Charter of the United Nations in relation to the

30 See also below, text to note 48; D.W. Bowett, "Estoppel before International Tribunals," 33 B.Y.I.L. (1957), p. 176 *et seq.;* I.C. MacGibbon, "Estoppel in International Law," 7 I.C.L.Q. (1958), p. 468 *et seq.;* Ch. Dominicé, *A propos du principe de l'estoppel en droit des gens, Mélanges Guggenheim* (1968), p. 327 *et seq.*, and , further, *loc cit.* above, note 19, p. 228 *et seq.*

31 See *above under* I and II(a).

32 See, further, *Vol I,* p. 453 *et seq.*, and *loc cit.* above, note 23, p. 110 et seq.

33 See also below under (8).

34 See,further, *Vol. I,* pp. 57, 448 and 491 *et seq.*, and *Vol. II,* p. 748 *et seq.*

35 See, further, *loc. cit.* above, note 23, p. 27 *et seq.*

good-faith branch of the *jus aequum* rule.[36]

(4) *Freedom of the seas.* In historical perspective, the rules of international customary law on the law of the seas are essentially the result of the interplay of the rules on recognition, consent and good faith with common sense and *tu quoque* considerations in states of peace, war and *status mixtus.*[37]

In the long run, most States refused to recognise extravagant claims of others to exclusive control over excessively large portions of the oceans. For a considerable time, they preferred to settle controversial issues over their rights in concrete situations in which some of them might be involved with each other or third States in relations of war or *status mixtus*. Thus again, prolonged experiments in treaty clauses and parallel practices provided the nourishing grounds out of which grew the laws and customs of maritime warfare and "pacific" blockade.

In any case, during the formative stages of these rules, the oceans were big enough to permit maritime Powers, on a basis of reciprocity, to be liberal about most uses of the high seas and treat them as permissible if not necessarily as reasonable. The *laissez-faire* attitudes taken by maritime Powers towards the legality under international customary law of overfishing to the point of extinction of whole species, pollution and nuclear tests, illustrate this proposition. Thus, also in this field, the *jus aequum* rule tends to be limited to its minimal, that is, good-faith, function.[38]

(5) *International responsibility.* This branch of international law owes more to the *jus aequum* rule than to any other law-shaping agency. It should, however, be remembered that in any rules on international responsibility it is assumed that, at least, one of the parties has acted contrary to its obligations under international customary or treaty law.

Treaty clauses, gradually transformed into rules of international customary law, and, again on a consensual basis, international judicial practice, have decisively moulded these rules by open resort to equitable consideration or, more often, behind thin conceptualist disguises. This applies as much to the conditions of the breach of international obligations, the requisites of legal interest in an international claim and the identity of the tortfeasor as the requirement of fault, the object and forms of reparation as to the forfeiture of claims by acquiescence (extinctive prescription).[39]

As with the presumption of good faith,[40] so the emphasis in some international judicial pronouncements on the subjective element in fault and the, on the surface, equitable aspects of the relevant rules on international

36 See above under I and below under (b).

37 For the reasons why, even so, it is advisable to classify rules under this head as rules belonging to the category of a fundamental principle of international customary law, see *loc. cit.* above, note 19, p. 365 *et seq.*

38 See above under (3) and below under (b), and, further, *loc. cit.* above, note 19, p. 212 *et seq.*

39 See, further, *Vol I,* p. 562 *et seq.,* and *loc. cit.* above, note 11, p. 101 *et seq.*

40 See above under (1).

responsibility actually tends to enlarge the spheres of sovereignty and international non-responsibility.[41]

(6) *Self-defence.* The evolution from a state of international law in which peace is but a consensual state of affairs to one in which self-defence and collective defence is the only justification of the threat and use of armed force has been a slow one. In theory, if not in practice, this process has been completed in international society organised on a confederate pattern in the United Nations.[42]

In the field of self-defence, little scope exists for the application of equitable considerations. Yet in at least one case, an international tribunal has considered the relevance of equitable considerations in relation to the law of reprisals, if not self-defence.

Under the international quasi-order of the League of Nations, it was controversial whether military reprisals remained lawful. Yet in the *Naulilaa Case* (1928), the German-Portuguese Arbitration Tribunal could ignore this aspect of the matter. It had to consider the legality of forcible German measures taken against Portugal in the alleged exercise of the right of reprisals during Portugal's neutrality in the First World War.

The Tribunal took it for granted that reprisals were limited by "considerations of humanity and the rules of good faith, applicable in the relations between States." What is more directly relevant from the point of view of equity is the further requirement, frequently postulated, of the proportional character of otherwise lawful reprisals.

The Tribunal recorded the divisions on this issue in the doctrine of international law but was not prepared to commit itself further than to condemn excessive reprisals.

It held that the reprisals taken by Germany against Portugal were excessive and, thus, illegal. Yet it also found that the first condition of lawful reprisals, that is, a preceding illegal act by Portugal, was not fulfilled. On the matter of excessive reprisals, the Tribunal's pronouncement was, therefore, merely *obiter.*[43]

Bearing in mind the difficulty of establishing the proportionality of non-identical military reprisals, there was wisdom in this attitude. It is easier to decide in a summary and impressionist way on what is clearly excessive rather than what is disproportionate. It is perhaps also more equitable to rely more on a qualitative, than a quantitative, test. Yet in the end, any such judgment is unavoidably subjective.

(7) *Good faith.* From its cradle in the law of treaties, good faith as the minimal content of equity has gradually overspilled into other fields of international customary law.

41 See also above under (1) and, further, *Vol. I,* p. 632 *et seq.*

42 See below under (b) and further, loc. cit. above, note 11, p. 234 *et seq.*, and *Vol. II,* p. 28 *et seq.*

43 United Nations, *Reports of International Arbitration Awards,* Vol. 2, p. 1011, at pp. 1025—1026, and, further, *Vol. II,* p. 48 *et seq.*

In view of the imperceptible way how, at one time or another, some rules of treaty law were taken for granted but continued to be applied in their former equitable content, it was—and is—difficult to judge accurately the scope of this permeation of international customary law by equity. Thus, it was tempting to proceed in more sweeping and speculative ways and rely on the elegance of broad moralising generalisations.

At least one illustration may be offered to convey the unreliability of a treatment of the subject in this vein. The issue of the legality of offers of bribery to enemy forces is to the point. It is a clear-cut situation. Such action is either lawful or unlawful. In the latter case, acts of attempted or successful bribery are subject to the extraordinary wartime jurisdiction of a belligerent over an alleged war criminal who has fallen into his hands, and to any civilised punishment from the death penalty downwards.[44]

It is generally accepted that, within limits, good faith must be observed between enemy Powers. Yet, in hostile relations, good faith tends to be reduced to its negative form and, for all purposes but transactions of a consensual character, means the absence of perfidy. The only question is the extent to which this moral rule has been incorporated in the laws and customs of war. In this respect, the treatment of the legality of bribery in military manuals and textbooks is instructive. Thus, in the 1936 version of Chapter XIV of the *British Manual of Military Law* the legality of bribery of enemy forces is justified on the ground that the belligerent can take measures to secure himself against such offences.[45] In other words, the matter is considered on an entirely amoral level: a belligerent may try to weaken the enemy as best he can, and it is for his enemy to guard himself to the best of his ability. In the 1958 edition of the United Kingdom *Manual of Military Law,* the previously offered justification is omitted altogether, and the legality of bribery justified by the illustration of a United Nations (United States) command offer made to the North Korean air force in the Korean War and a cross-reference to the latest edition of Oppenheim's *International Law* which itself had gone through significant changes in emphasis on the subject.[46]

In fields of international law subject to the application of the rules on good faith,[47] the breach of good faith creates an estoppel. This means a situation in which a party is not permitted to take any action incompatible with its own previous behaviour or declaration (prohibition of *venire contra factum proprium*). Thus, in the *Chorzów Factory (Jurisdiction) Case* (1927), the Permanent Court of International Justice held it to be a

44 See, further, *ibid.* p. 478 *et seq.*

45 Para. 144 (*Manual of Military Law 1929,* Amendment No. 12 (1936), p. 34).
Compare also para. 38 of the United States War Department Basic Field Manual on the *Rules of Land Warfare* (1940), p. 10, with para. 49 of the United States Department of the Army Field Manual on *The Law of Land Warfare* (1956), p. 22.

46 Paragraph 313 (p. 102). See, further, *Transactions of the Grotius Society,* Vol. 42 (1957), p. 166, note 48.

47 See below under (8).

"principle generally accepted in the jurisprudence of international arbitration as well as by municipal courts that one Party cannot avail himself of the fact that the other has not fulfilled some obligation or has not had recourse to some means of redress, if the former party has, by some illegal act, prevented the latter from fulfilling the obligation in question, or from having recourse to the tribunal which would have been open to him."[48]

In particular on the international judicial level, it is estoppel which regulates the relations between international and municipal law. An international court such as the International Court of Justice is bound to give priority to international law over municipal law because of its own subjection to Article 38 of its Statute. Similarly, parties before the Court are subject to this law. Thus they also are estopped from arguing that their own constitutions or any of their State organs prevent them from complying with international law.[49]

(8) *Functions of good faith.* The rules of international customary law which can be inductively substantiated and justify the abstraction from them of good faith as one of the seven fundamental principles of international law can be summarised under four heads:

(1) (a) Parties to consensual engagements must interpret and execute such engagements in good faith.

(b) Within the limits of their binding character, the same duties arise in the case of duly communicated unilateral acts.

(c) If a consensual engagement which is subject to ratification is actually ratified, good faith regulates the rights and duties of the contracting parties during the interval between signature and ratification and, sometimes, even further back.

(d) In the absence of provisions of a more specialised character, acts contrary to good faith on the part of an international institution, which itself derives its authority from a consensual engagement, are void.

(2) Within limits to be ascertained from the actual contents of each particular rule, such rules of international customary law as form part of *jus aequum* must be interpreted as relative rights.

(3) Other rules of international customary law are to be interpreted as absolute rights of *jus strictum* or in accordance with the ethical minimum standards laid down specifically in such rules. Their arbitrary or unreasonable exercise is not illegal, but amounts to an unfriendly act.

(4) On the international judicial level, absolute rights tend to be transformed into relative rights in the course of a balancing process in

48 Series A. No. 9, p. 31.

49 See, further, *Vol I,* p. 67 *et seq.,* and, on the relativist theory of the relations between international and municipal law, Diagram No. 6 in the writer's *Manual of International Law* (1967), p. 48.

which considerations of good faith and reasonableness play a prominent part.[50]

In previous sections, the impact of the rules underlying the principle of good faith on those governing other fundamental principles and the interplay of these rules has been illustrated. In all these cases, the rules on good faith fulfil a relativising function. They transform absolute legal rights into relative rights behind quasi-legal and quasi-logical façades, they temper the exercise of judicial discretion and contribute to an organic growth of the rules of international law. More clearly than any other rules, those on the interpretation of treaties and international responsibility bear witness to this dynamic function of good faith in the system of international law.

These processes operate continuously not only on the level of the primary rules of international law, that is, those directly sustaining the seven fundamental principles of international law, but also on that of the secondary rules which are the products of the interplay between the primary rules. It must suffice to draw attention to two of the most important sets of secondary rules of international law: those on territory[51] and internal armed conflict.[52]

(b) *Equity in organised international society*

Illustrations have been offered of the change in emphasis from absolute rights in partly organised international society as, for instance, on the international judicial level in pre-1914 international society.

Three factors exceptionally favour the application of the *jus aequum* rule on the international judicial level: the consensual basis of the jurisdiction of all international arbitral and judicial organs; the duties of good faith which this treaty basis imposes on the parties in their relations with each other and the tribunal, and on the arbitrators and judges themselves, and, finally, the discretion which, by implication, parties grant to such judicial organs to engage in subtle, and largely undisclosed, balancing processes between potentially applicable rules.[53]

If, as in the League of Nations or United Nations, international society itself is organised on the basis of a multilateral treaty and furnished with institutions of its own, these relativising trends in international law are powerfully strengthened.

A summary survey of the potentialities and limitations of *jus aequum* on this confederate level is all that it is possible to offer in this Chapter.

To facilitate comparison, the illustrations selected will be grouped

50 On this last rule, see, further, below under (b).
51 See, further, *Vol. I*, p. 289 *et seq.*
52 See, further, *Vol. II*, p. 673 *et seq.*
53 See, further, *loc. cit.* above, note 20, *Inductive Approach*, (1965), pp. 141-143, and note 23, p. 106 *et seq.*

under the headings of the seven fundamental principles of international customary law discussed above.[54]

(1) *Sovereignty.* In at least three places in the Charter of the United Nations, the principle of sovereign equality is re-emphasised. Yet, by the insertion of this principle in a multilateral treaty, the rights and duties arising under the head of sovereign equality themselves become subject to the *jus aequum* rule and have to be balanced equitably against the other obligations of member States.[55]

It is also noteworthy that, in the Vienna Conventions of 1961 and 1963 on Diplomatic and Consular Relations, prepared under the auspices of the United Nations, the absolute right of receiving States to declare a diplomatic or consular representative accredited to them to be *persona non grata* has been preserved unimpaired.[56] This is a significant re-emphasis on *jus strictum* in organised international society.

(2) *Recognition.* The divergencies in the policies of individual members of the United Nations regarding the recognition of the Peking or Taiwan (Formosa) regime as the government of mainland China and the recognition of the governments of divided States such as Germany, Korea and Vietnam prove that discretion continues to reign supreme in this field.[57]

In a minor way, the results of membership in the United Nations of one of these regimes—and the same applies to States not recognised by some other member States, as for instance, Israel—affect non-recognition policies. If one of these States is a member of the United Nations or one of the governments competing in a member State is represented in the organs of the United Nations, even member States which have not recognised such a State or government must treat the representatives of the State concerned as if they had done so. At least this is so for all purposes connected with the United Nations. This is the result of the estoppel created by the admission of such a State to membership and its government to the various organs of the United Nations.[58]

(3) *Consent.* Some of the relevant points—embodiment of the principles of good faith and good neighbourliness in the Charter of the United Nations—have been made in another context.[59]

The creation of *jus strictum* on a higher level than that of *jus aequum* under international customary law is another striking example of the variations available in consensual law-making.

Thus, the Geneva Conventions of 1929 and 1949 for the Protection of

[54] See above under (a).

[55] See, further, *loc. cit.* above, note 23, p. 78 *et seq.*

[56] Art. 9 of the Vienna Convention on Diplomatic Relations, October 31, 1961 (Cmnd. 2565-1965) and Art. 23 of the Vienna Convention on Consular Relations, April 24, 1963 (Cmnd. 2113/1963).
See also above, text to note 29.

[57] See above under (a) (2) and, further, *loc, cit.* above, note 23, pp. 267 and 272 *et seq.*

[58] See, further, *Vol. I,* pp. 51-52, 95 and 127 *et seq.*, and *Vol II,* pp. 48, 490 and 327 *et seq.*

[59] See above under I.

War Victims contain "in all circumstances" clauses, for instance, in relation to the basic duties under Article 3 in all four 1949 Conventions.

These clauses not only provide consensual *jus cogens* from which the parties may not derogate by way of agreements among some of them, but also consensual *jus strictum.*

It is the purpose of this *jus strictum* to make the treaty commitments which are subject to "in all circumstances" clauses, absolute and exclude justifications and excuses of non-compliance with these obligations which, otherwise, would be admissible under *jus aequum.*[60].

(4) *Freedom of the seas.* In view of the wide range of Article 2 of the Convention on the High Seas, it is permissible to single out this Article from other clauses of *jus aequum* in the 1958 Conventions on the law of the sea. It is postulated in Article 2 that the freedoms of the seas enumerated in this Article and others which are recognised by the general principles of international law shall be exercised by all States "with reasonable regard" to the interests of other States in their exercise of the freedom of the high seas.[61]

Similarly, regarding the freedom to lay submarine cables and pipelines, it was necessary to establish priorities in relation to the right of the coastal State to explore its continental shelf and exploit its natural resources. Again, the test of reasonableness provided the answer.[62]

It proved, however, impossible to induce the Contracting Parties to extend the test of reasonable use to the question of the pollution of the high seas. The draftsmen of the Convention had to content themselves with more modest clauses on the pollution of the seas by the discharge of oil from enumerated sources and dumping of nuclear waste, leaving the matter otherwise with the States concerned and conventions to be subsequently concluded.[63]

(5) *International responsibility.* The most remarkable developments in the field of international responsibility which are relevant from the point of view of equity are in the sphere of international war crimes jurisdiction. In admitting defences, the International Military Tribunals of Nuremberg and Tokyo were limited by their Charters.

Both Charters went further in this respect than international customary law required.[64] While, in the Charters of both Tribunals, the plea of superior orders was excluded as a justification, it was admitted as a plea in

60 See, further, *Vol II,* pp. 129, 238, 350, 456, 633 and 718, and the Advisory Opinion of the International Court of Justice in the *Namibia (South-West Africa) Case, I.C.J. Reports 1971,* p. 47.

61 Cmnd. 584 (1958), p. 27.
See also above note 17.

62 Art. 26 (*ibid.* p. 32).

63 See, further, E.D. Brown, *The Legal Regime of Hydrospace* (1971), Chap. 4, and *loc, cit.* above, note 23, pp. 100 et seq. and 214.

64 See, further, *Vol. II,* p. 478 *et seq.*

mitigation of punishment.[65] What is more significant is that the Tribunals used their judicial discretion to introduce other equitable considerations in favour of the accused: restrictive interpretation of the clauses on conspiracy to wage aggressive war and on criminal organisations[66] and mitigating circumstances on which the Charters of the Tribunals remained silent.[67]

(6) *Self-defence.* Under the Charter of the United Nations, the relation between the prohibition of the threat and use of force under Paragraph 4 of Article 2 and the legality of armed self-defence and collective defence against armed attack is controversial.[68] Yet is is probably more in accordance with the intention of the Contracting Parties to interpret Article 51, together with Articles 53, 106 and 107, as the only permissible exceptions to this rule.

Thus, as with the rules governing sovereignty, the "inherent" right of self-defence has been tamed. In the context of the Charter of the United Nations, it must be interpreted in a spirit of *jus aequum.* Such doubts as arise on the practical relevance of this interpretation have little to do with "inherent" difficulties of testing action by reference to *jus aequum* but a great deal with the structural weakness of the United Nations. In too many cases, these shortcomings leave decisions in a state of auto-interpretation by the parties involved.[69]

(7) *Good faith.* The incorporation of the principle of good faith in the Charter of the United Nations has been noted earlier.[70]

Yet another task waited to be performed. The number and size of the international administrative services of the United Nations and its Specialised Agencies had expanded at an unprecedented rate. Thus the internal law of these consensual superstructures was in need of drastic adjustment to the minimum conditions of the rule of law for more adequate protection of the staff of these organisations.

Following in the footsteps of the League of Nations, the contracts of these international civil servants and their conditions of service were made amenable to a measure of judicial control, a new chapter of equity in action. In this way, some checks were imposed on the possibility of

65 See, for instance, Y. Dinstein, *The Defence of "Obedience to Superior Orders" in International Law* (1965) and, further, *Vol. II,* p. 516 *et seq.*

66 See, further, *Vol II,* p. 499 *et seq.*

67 See, further, *ibid,* p. 520 *et seq.*

68 See, further, *loc. cit.* above, note 19, p. 335 *et seq.*

69 See, further, *Vol II,* pp. 50 *et seq.* and 539-540, and *loc. cit.* above, note 20 (1965), pp. 184-185.

70 See above under I, and also the Declaration on Principles of International Law concerning Friendly Relations and Co-operation among States, etc. (Gen. Ass. Res. 2625 (XXV) of October 24, 1970): "Sovereign equality includes the following elements: ... (f) Each State has the duty to comply fully and in good faith with its international obligations" and *ibid.* the further elaboration of the principle of good faith.

abuse of discretionary powers in the higher echelons of these institutions.[71]

(c) *Equity in supranational institutions*

An even richer yield than in the internal law of international institutions on the confederate level is to be gathered from the practice of the organs of supranational institutions, especially that of the Court of Justice of the European Communities.[72]

In these Communities, we enter the border zone of functional federalism. Here, as in mature territorial federations or unitary States, we may expect to find a considerable measure of *jus aequum*.

So long as supranational commitments are based on treaty law, they can legitimately be adduced as evidence of international law. Yet a word of warning may be appropriate on the dangers of using this material in an unscientific way. It is legitimate to argue from lower to higher levels of international organisation. Thus, in the *Donauversickerung Case* (1927), it was properly argued before the German *Verfassungsgericht* that, at least in the relations between federal States, the same duties of *jus aequum* applied as between sovereign States under international customary law.[73]

What is unacceptable is the reversal of this argument, that is, the use of *jus aequum*, as developed on higher levels of international organisation, as precedents to be applied on lower levels of international integration.

CONCLUSIONS

It remains to check how far the working hypotheses set out in earlier

71 See, further, the Advisory Opinion on *Judgments of the Administrative Tribunal of the ILO, I.C.J. Reports 1956*, pp. 91-97; *Aubert and Others v. Secretary-General of the United Nations* (1950), *Judgments of the United Nations Administrative Tribunal 1950—1957* (1958), p. 4; *Crawford v. The same* (1953), *ibid*, p. 68; *Khavkine v. The same* (1956), *ibid. p. 382. See also L.C. Green, "The Status of the International Civil Service," 7 C.L.P. (1954), p. 192 et seq.;* J.E.S. Fawcett, "Détournement de pourvoir by International Organisations," 35 B.Y.I.L. (1957), p. 311 *et seq.*; C.W. Jenks, *The Proper Law of International Organisations* (1962), p. 25 *et seq.;* A.H. Schechter, *Interpretation of Ambiguous Documents by International Administrative Tribunals.* (1964), p. 49 *eq set.*; E. Schwelb, *The Abuse of the Right of Petition* (3 RDH-H.R.J., 1970) and *Vol. III* p. 449 *eq seq.*

See also *Lachmueller and Others* v. *E.E.C. Commission, Recueil de la Jurisprudence de la Cour de Justice des Communautés Européennes*, Vol. 6 (1960), p. 933, at p. 956: "Attendu que l'action de l'autorité, dans le domaine administratif comme dans le domaine contractuel, est toujours soumise au respect du principe de la bonne foi."

72 For relevant judgments in nullity proceedings under Art. 33 of the Treaty of 1951 on the European Coal and Steel Community on the ground of misuse of powers, under Art. 173 of the Treaty of 1957 on the European Economic Community and Art. 146 of the Treaty of 1957 on the European Atomic Energy Community, see G. Bebr, *Judicial Control of the European Communities* (1962), p. 33 *et seq.;* D.C. Valentine, *The Court of Justice of the European Communities*, Vol. I (1965), pp. 138, 287 and 363 *et seq.;* A.W. Green, *Political Integration by Jurisprudence* (1969), p. 87 *et seq.* See also 16 C.L.P. (1963), p. 22 *et seq.*

73 *Entscheidungen des Reichsgerichts in Zivilsachen*, Vol. 116, Appendix, p. 18, at pp. 31—32.

See, further, *Vol. I*, p. 220, *Vol III*, p. 387 *et seq.*, and *loc. cit.* above, note 19, pp. 291-293.

sections of this Chapter[74] require to be modified and put the conclusions reached in coherent order:

(1) *Jus aequum* in its minimal, essentially negative and, in sociological terminology, society sense, means good faith, as distinct from perfidy and evasion of legal obligations. Its function is to assist in preventing a relapse into anarchy or order without law.

Jus aequum in its positive, and community, sense means infusing considerations of reasonableness and good faith into legal relations and taking good faith in its negative meaning for granted.

(2) The chief function of *jus aequum* in its positive sense is to transform absolute rights into relative rights and thus to smooth the interplay of the rules of international law.

(3) While, in unorganised international society, good faith has primarily a negative meaning, on an initially consensual basis it has acquired a more positive meaning in a number of fields, especially those of treaty law and international responsibility.

(4) In relation to each rule of international customary law it requires concrete verification whether, and to what extent, good faith and *jus aequum* in its wider meaning of common sense and reasonableness have been received into international law.

(5) Owing to the consensual basis of all international arbitral and judicial jurisdiction, international law as applied by international courts and tribunals tends to be applied in a spirit of *jus aequum*.

(6) Subjects of international law remain free to enter commitments *juris stricti* and reduce *jus aequum* to its minimal function. Similarly, they may transform the *jus aequum* rule or any of its façets into rules of consensual *jus cogens*.

(7) Corresponding to the evolution of international societies from a state of non-organisation to organisation on confederate and supranational levels, international *jus aequum* tends to acquire a positive meaning and realise its highest potential.

74 See above, Introduction, and under I (c).

Chapter 5

THE LAW OF ARMED CONFLICT: A CIVILISED INTERLUDE?

"The General Assembly ... decides to include in the provisional agenda of its thirtieth session the item entitled 'Urgent need for cessation of nuclear and thermonuclear tests and conclusion of a treaty designed to achieve a comprehensive test ban'." U.N. General Assembly *Resolution 3257 (XXIX), December 9, 1974.*

A traditional view of the evolution of the laws and customs of war or as it may be preferable to term them the law of armed conflict, is expressed, in substance unaltered since 1914, in the various editions of the British *Manual of Military Law* (latest edition 1958). The contemporary law of armed conflict is essentially the product of three formative factors behind the law: complusion, humanity and chivalry.

Thus, in principle, belligerents are entitled to apply against each other all means of *compulsion,* including force of any kind, which are required to attain the strategic object of warfare. This object is complete submission of the enemy at the earliest possible moment, with the least possible expenditure of men, resources and money.

In this context, the dictates of *humanity* prohibit any use of unnecessary violence, and the canons of *chivalry* demand a certain amount of fairness in offence and defence, and some degree of mutual respect between the opposing forces.

The decisive question is: In what proportions are these frequently incompatible principles to be applied? From this point of view, the changes made in successive editions of the British *Manual of Military Law* or, for that matter, in the military manuals of other countries such as the United States of America, are instructive.

In the laws of war in the narrower sense, that is, the rules applicable in actual combat zones, as distinct from territories under belligerent occupation and home territories of belligerents, the unlimited use of the most effective means of destroying enemy foces is accepted. For instance, short of limitations imposed by international conventions, the legality of the use of flamethrowers, napalm bombs and nuclear weapons, as well as chemical and biological warfare in general is uncompromisingly asserted in the United States Army Field Manual on *The Law of Land Warfare* (1956). In the United Kingdom Manual of 1958, however, reservations are made, for instance, regarding chemical warfare. The application of such, in themselves illegal, weapons is considered to be permissible as a reprisal against enemies whose allies resort to the use of these weapons.

In effect, the application of considerations of humanity and civilisation is essentially limited to war victims. This is how, in the *Geneva Conventions of 1949* (Cmnd. 550, 1958), wounded and sick members of armed forces, prisoners of war and civilian persons in enemy and enemy-occupied territories are described. In a terminology in vogue in the International Committee of the Red Cross, this part of the Law of Armed Conflict has also been called the humanitarian law of war.

To cope adequately with controversial issues such as the legality of saturation bombing and nuclear weapons, the position of guerrilleros and the application of the Law of Armed Conflict to wars such as those in Korea, Nigeria, Pakistan, Vietnam and Laos, it is advisable to view these problems in a commensurate historical perspective.

In this context a distinction drawn by R.G. Collingwood in a masterly work *(The New Leviathan,* 1942), written on his deathbed, deserves to be recalled. It is the threefold distinction between savagery, civilisation and barbarism.

Savagery is the state of a group before it attains *civilisation* of a sort, that is, a minimum of relations on a footing of free and spontaneous co-operation, rather than compulsion, for commonly accepted purposes. If, subsequently, a civilised community relapses into a state comparable to pristine savagery, this he terms *barbarism.*

To obtain a reasonably clear picture of the functions and limitations of the Law of Armed Conflict, it is proposed to examine in this Chapter the impact of the Law of Armed Conflict on social groups in the three categories of savagery, civilisation and barbarism.

I—SAVAGE WARFARE

In *The Beginnings of Diplomacy* (1950), R. Numelin assembles the contradictory and, quantitatively, inconclusive evidence on the normality of war as an institution in a savage society.

One conclusion appears to emerge from this material which, perhaps, is slightly weighted in favour of the peaceful character of that idealised figure of eighteenth-century Western literature: the noble savage. It is that, in inter-tribal relations in which war occurs exceptionally or otherwise, there is no differentiation between customary, religious and legal duties. In inter-tribal as in internal tribal relations, custom reigns supreme.

The anthropological material available indicates considerable diversities in the behaviour of different ethnic groups and in different parts of the world. In the Pacific area, and among the Eskimos, war as a social institution for the forceful solution of communal conflicts was less frequent than among European and other Aryan savages.

Moreover, in any generalisation regarding the standards of behaviour observed by communities in early stages of civilisation, a distinction must be drawn. Restraints, for instance, in treating women and children, may have applied between related tribes but did not necessarily apply between, for instance, immigrant Hottentots and dwarf tribes of local bushmen they encountered.

Moreover, the relative similarities, rather than differences, between all surviving human races lend some credence to the hypothesis that the pristine ancestors of all of them must have practised policies of wholesale extermination or "genocide" of hominoids and hominids in their migrations and areas of settlement.

Thus, for purposes of tracing the origins of the Law of Armed Conflict, speculations on the intrinsically peaceful or aggressive character of *homo habilis,* probably misdescribed by anthropologists as *homo sapiens,* are largely immaterial. It may be taken for granted that man, and in lawyer's fashion this includes woman, is shaped in his peaceful or aggressive behaviour by his environment rather than innate characteristics. Even so, enough evidence exists in favour of the thesis of the predominance in the evolution of international society of the pattern of *homo homini lupus.* At least in international relations there has been a prevalence of society attitudes, as distinct from community attitudes, and sovereign States tend to behave towards each other as wolves, rather than lions, peacefully co-existing with the lambs of international society.

While the frequency of wars in some inter-group relations of savage tribes may differ, the existence of war as a social pattern in savage society must be accepted. It is likely that, in extreme cases, war between savage tribes was waged as it is still waged in our time between some South American jungle tribes. What this means is pictured in *Yanoama* (Allen and Unwin, London, 1971), Helena Valero's autobiographical story (retold by E. Biocca) of her life since her capture as a child by the Yanoama Indians. In an unforgettable passage, she records what happened when, in the frontier land between Brazil and Venezuela, former allies attacked her captors and took some of the band's women and children prisoner:

"Meanwhile from all sides the women continued to arrive with their children, whom the other Karawetari had captured. They all joined us. Then the men began to kill the children; the little ones, bigger ones, they killed many of them. They tried to run away, but they caught them, and threw them on the ground, and stuck them with bows, which went through their bodies and rooted them to the ground. Taking the smallest by the feet, they beat them against the trees and rocks. The children's eyes trembled. Then the men took the dead bodies and threw them among the rocks, saying: 'Stay there, so that your fathers can find you and eat you.' They killed so many. I was weeping for fear and for pity, but there was nothing I could do. They snatched the children from their mothers to kill them, while the others held the mothers tightly by the arms and wrists as they stood up in a line."

The behaviour of the twentieth-century savages in the Orinoco basin has its analogies in other instances of recorded history. It reminds us of the wars of total annihilation waged against some of their enemies by the Israelite invaders of the Promised Land (1 Samuel 15.3 *et seq.*) and the pyramids of skulls left behind by the Mongol hordes.

In other instances, as among savage tribes in former New Guinea or what in United Nations parlance has become West Irian, savage warfare may be largely ritualised and more restrained than a European or American football match. Even so, whatever restraints were or are practised in savage warfare are of a non-legal character. They share with any Law of Armed Conflict but the feature of establishing inhibitions against carnage unlimited.

II—CIVILISED WARFARE

Beyond the distinction drawn between civilisation, savagery and barbarism, three further aspects of the phenomenon of civilisation are relevant for purposes of the Law of Armed Conflict:

(1) As, again, Collingwood has pointed out, the term "civilisation" has different meanings in relation to nature and in relation to man. While, in relation to nature, it means intelligent exploitation, in relation to man, it means spontaneous co-operation.

(2) Civilisation is a dynamic phenomenon. It tends to move forward to fuller co-operation or backward to more complete exploitation of man by his fellow-men. Thus, in any particular phase of history, no group is likely to be entirely civilised or uncivilised but more or less civilised.

(3) The, often, dynamic character of the movement towards or from civilisation makes it unlikely that, on a world scale, only one civilisation exists at any particular time. Actually, we know from archaeology and comparative history how many civilisations have come and gone in the continuous struggle of *homo habilis* to raise himself out of the primordial state of savagery to the state ever denied to him of becoming the mortal god. This is the meaning of the biblical images of the leviathan, the monster, half man and half beast, rising from the waters with crown, sceptre and sword, and behemoth, the powerful beast of the land who is the "chief of the ways of God". It is significant that Thomas Hobbes likened the one to the sovereign State (*Leviathan* (1651)) and chose the other as the title of his less known work on the history of the causes of the civil wars of England from 1640 to 1660 (*Behemoth*-1682).

Yet the plurality of civilisations co-existing with one another is compatible with the predominance of one or some over the rest. This explains why, in an unprecedented technological expansion during the nineteenth century, Western civilisation became—at least for a time—the world's leading civilisation, and how Western international law achieved its universality.

Moreover, the organisation of international societies of the past and present in overriding systems of open power politics and power politics in disguise must be recalled. This factor, together with the exclusiveness, dynamism and co-existence of civilisations, makes it easier to understand the slender character of the limitations imposed by law on the rule of force in international relations.

(a) *Law-Conditioning Factors*

In this context, perhaps the most significant aspect of total warfare as waged by the Israelite invaders of Canaan against some of their enemies was not its indiscriminate character but the need felt in religious quarters for justification of these wars of extermination by God's command.

The emergence of other nations from savagery to civilisation is accompanied by comparable distinctions between nations against which, in principle, they practised unlimited warfare and others to whom they meted out a more humane treatment. Thus, subject to exceptions to be considered, Romans and Greeks alike imposed limitations on their warfare against nations akin to themselves. Yet they neither expected nor gave quarter otherwise than their own self-interest dictated to nations whom they considered to be mere barbarians. Similarly, in warfare among themselves, the light-skinned invaders of India paid some respect to considerations of justice and equity—the oversold notion of *dharma* in Indian post-independence literature. Yet few of these restraints were shown to their dark-skinned predecessors who were exterminated or pushed further into Southern India.

In a retrospective rationalisation of this double-standard practice, Greeks, Romans and Indians alike treated those whom they considered to be barbarians not as fellow-humans but as part of nature to be used as they saw fit. When Cicero described slaves as animated things (*res animata*), he employed a similar ideology.

The treatment of defeated enemies on a basis of mere self-interest and reason of State found its classic expression in the fate of barbarian leaders who were dragged along in the triumphal processions of victorious Roman generals. When these captives had served their purpose, they were unceremoniously executed. For the rest, the profit motive recommended the enslavement of the vanquished, rather than their indiscriminate slaughter.

In Western medieval warfare, the circle of those who could expect civilised treatment was even more narrowly drawn. The Church enjoined rulers in inter-Christian warfare to spare priests, women and children. Yet these canons of chivalry and mercy did not prevent the pillage, raping, burning and killing that formed a traditional part of, for instance, the Anglo-French wars of the Middle Ages or the Anglo-Scots border wars.

The relativity of the meaning of civilisation is further demonstrated by the indiscriminate slaughter in the Crusades and the religious wars in the Europe of the sixteenth and seventeenth centuries; the "frontier" wars waged by the white trappers and settlers against the Indians in North America, and the man-hunts against Indians in South and Central America and bushmen in Australia and South Africa.

While the, on the whole, restraining influence of the Christian churches on warfare should be acknowledged, two other factors, operating in the same direction, deserve greater emphasis. During the period of mercenary warfare in the Renaissance, the trade union attitudes of mercenaries—and, subsequently, the needs of absolutist rulers to buy their cannon fodder—led to greater appreciation of soldiers as an expensive commodity.

Moreover, as is proved by the elaborate codification of Articles of War in most European countries—the first English Ordinance for the Government of the Army was issued in 1386 by Richard II—generals rediscovered another truth. If, after a victory in the field or the surrender of a fortified place, they failed to control their troops or settle in advance the fate of prisoners of war and war booty, their armies were likely to disintegrate into undisciplined rabbles and become useless as instruments of warfare.

The most that can be said in favour of the trends limiting the application of force is that they led to a continuous tug-of-war between the requirements of the standard of civilisation and military necessities.

Yet whenever military necessities seriously came in conflict with moral or other restraints which make up the standard of civilisation, military necessities tended to prevail. In particular, this applied whenever a new weapon was less humane than its predecessor but surpassed it in destructive power or terrorising effects. It was only the Chinese who, for centuries, refrained from using explosives in warfare because of the excessive destructiveness and inhumanity of these weapons.

(b) *The Equilibrium in the pre-1914 Laws of War*

Before the First World War, the antinomy between military necessities and the standard of civilisation resulted in a relatively stable equilibrium. In wars between civilised nations, five legally relevant distinctions were accepted:

(1) *The distinction between international and internal war.* International law is concerned only with armed conflicts between subjects of international law. Normally this means sovereign States but, exceptionally, this includes abnormal types of groups such as dependent States.

In principle, internal wars remain within the exclusive jurisdiction of the State involved. If an internal war is prolonged, and revolutionaries or other rebels are effectively in control of considerable areas of the State concerned, practice has made minor inroads into the rule of the prohibition of intervention by foreign States in an internal war. Third States may recognise such revolutionaries as belligerents or insurgents and, while these actually fulfil governmental and administrative functions in part of a State's territory, treat them as if they were the authorities of an independent State. To this extent, in the relations between third States and revolutionaries so recognised, the rules of the law of neutrality apply.

The only difference between the recognition of revolutionaries as belligerents, such as the recognition by Great Britain of the Southern Confederation during the American Civil War (1861-65), and the recognition of revolutionaries as insurgents is one of the scope of recognition. If revolutionaries are recognised as belligerents, they may exercise all the rights of belligerents anywhere, including the high seas. If they are recognised merely as insurgents, their recognition is limited to the territory, including the territorial sea, of the State disrupted by internal war.

(2) *The distinction between members of armed forces and civilians.* The governing rules enable a belligerent to sort out the goats from the sheep in areas under his wartime occupation. While the former are liable to the restraints that may be imposed on prisoners of war, the latter may expect a modicum of rule of law in enemy-occupied territories.

(3) *The distinction between combatants and non-combatants.* Combatants are legitimate objects of enemy action. Thus they must except the application against themselves of all the rigours of war. They are protected by but few rules of international law which impose limitations on the freedom of the enemy to kill, maim and capture them. The rule prohibiting the use of poison and poisoned weapons is one of the rare cases in which, in the relations between combatants, the standard of civilisation prevails over the necessities of war.

Non-combatants as such are not legitimate objects of war. If they are members of armed forces, they may be put under restraint but, as non-combatants, they are entitled to the protection of the relevant rules of international customary law and the Geneva Conventions of 1906, 1929 and 1949.

If enemy non-combatants are civilians, their status depends on their own behaviour. If, before their capture, they have acted as combatants without being members of enemy armed forces or units assimilated to such armed forces by international coventions, they are not protected by the laws of war or these Conventions. The enemy's freedom of action is limited merely by minimal requirements of the standard of civilisation, which are codified in Article 3 of the four Geneva Conventions of 1949.

If such civilians are genuine non-combatants, they receive the wider protection granted to civilians in areas other than combat zones by the laws of war and relevant conventions, especially Geneva Convention IV of 1949 on the Protection of Civilians in Time of War.

(4) *The distinction between laws of war in the wider and narrower senses.* Pre-1914 international law affirms that the right of belligerents to adopt means of injuring the enemy is not unlimited. Yet in actual combat on land and at sea, such limitations of the freedom of action of belligerents as exist impose few restraints on the conduct of land and sea operations. In the laws of war in this narrower sense, military necessities generally remain overriding.

Yet, by the introduction of functional distinctions such as those between combatants and non-combatants, privileged and unprivileged prisoners of war, ships which are good prize and others which are immune from capture, and combat zones and areas under belligent occupation, a law of war in a wider sense has developed. The practice of national prize courts, essentially but not exclusively concerned with the protection of neutral ships and cargo, and the law of belligerent occupation offer evidence of the technical sophistication attained in these branches of the Law of Armed Conflict.

(5) *The distinction between belligerents and neutrals.* Like the distinction between international and internal war, that between belligerent and neutral States tends to limit armed conflicts. In pre-1914 international law, the major rights and duties of neutral States in relation to belligerents may be summarised as the right to inviolability of neutral territory and the duties of impartiality and abstention of neutral Powers. Yet, especially in the law of maritime neutrality, a good many major issues remained unsettled.

(c) *Forms and Working Principles of the Law of Armed Conflict*

The evolution of the pre-1914 Law of Armed Conflict went through four phases: the *Articles of War phase,* with primary emphasis on the disciplinary aspects of breaches of the laws of war; the *Manual phase* during which military textbooks served as much to advertise the civilised standards which the authorities issuing these manuals had attained as to influence the actual behaviour of the military; the *codification phase,* when, during the Hague Peace Conferences of 1899 and 1907, governments tried to placate an increasingly restive public opinion by codification of parallel national practices or compromises between national policies in international conventions, and an overlapping and still continuing *development phase* when, under the impact of similar and equally complex motivations, Governments deliberated, and go on deliberating, at diplomatic conclaves whether and how the existing laws of war can be improved.

In historical perspective, the pre-1914 laws of war and neutrality were vastly superior to the rudimentary rules of preceding periods. The working principle behind these rules was that of reciprocity, employed positively within a generally accepted political framework. This was the international quasi-order that was constituted by the pre-1914 system of an international balance of power. So long as the majority of the Powers were prepared to work on this footing, war was a continuation of politics by other means, but such trials of strength would not necessarily get out of hand. As belligerents or neutrals, all concerned continued to treat each other as respected members of the same civilisation, and any unnecessary use of force or wanton acts of cruelty would merely impede the peace settlement that eventually would have to be made.

Similarly, if belligerents failed to respect the neutrality of non-belligerents, they would be likely to push neutral States into the opposite belligerent camp and transform a duel war into a general war.

For analogous reasons, internal wars had to be confined. If other States became involved in internal wars. these might develop into general wars, and, in the end, such general wars might not be confined to the overthrow of a particular system of balance of power. They might produce a state of anarchy in which it might prove difficult to re-establish any new system of balance of power and maintain the existing social order in any of the States concerned.

Thus, a reasonably humane law of armed conflict which left every State free to resort to war (*jus ad bellum*) and merely restrained its armed forces in the conduct of war *(jus in bello)* was well suited to the needs of pre-1914 international power politics. It enabled the governments of the Powers to present themselves to public opinion at home and abroad as wary but civilised guardians of the national weal.

III—THE CHALLENGE OF NEO-BARBARISM

In the period between the First and Second World Wars, the work of the codification and development of the laws of war continued in a half-hearted manner. Believers in collective security considered the whole body of the traditional laws of war and neutrality to be dated and concern with the laws of war a lack of faith in collective action.

Yet, the attempts made in the Covenant of the League of Nations to limit resort to war left open so many loopholes for resort to armed force that this agrument was self-defeating. In any case, the League of Nations never achieved a sufficient degree of universality to give credibility to its system of collective security on a global scale. Moreover, the piecemeal application of economic sanctions in the Italo-Ethiopian War proved that, by 1936, more was amiss with the collective system of the League of Nations than its lack of universality.

The Kellogg Pact (1928) by which war as a means of national policy was outlawed achieved near-universality. Experience proved quickly, however, that, in the absence of an effective international order behind the law, this Treaty could be broken with apparent impunity. Even so, the Pact was useful in providing, at last, a test of the lawfulness of resort to war. Until then, this object had been achieved only in the most formal sense. Parties to Hague Convention III of 1907 had to declare war or issue a conditional ultimatum in writing. Otherwise pre-1914 State practice, as distinct from vague distinctions between just and unjust wars made by naturalist writers, treated offensive and defensive war as equally legal.

Under pressure from public opinion, an International Commission for the Revision of the Rules of Warfare drew up some Rules on Air Warfare (1923). In these an attempt was made to limit lawful bombing from the air to military objectives. Yet these Rules never came into operation.

In 1925, a Protocol on the Prohibition of the Use in War of Asphyxiating, Poisonous or other Gases and of Bacteriological Methods of Warfare was adopted. Most parties to the Convention considered the Protocol to be merely declaratory of existing law, but the United States of America, who signed but did not then ratify the Protocol, treated it as a development of the laws of war and, thus, not as binding on non-parties.

In 1929, the International Committee of the Red Cross succeeded in inducing the Powers to agree to inconspicuous but useful improvements in two conventions on the Amelioration of the Condition of Wounded and Sick in Armed Forces in the Field and on Prisoners of War.

On the surface, substantial progress was made in the final stages of the Second World War. In the Charter of the United Nations, the outlawry of resort to war was extended to the threat and use of force but subject to important limitations (Articles 2(4), 51, 53, 103 and 107 of the Charter).

In 1947 the General Assembly of the United Nations unanimously adopted the Nuremberg Principles. Thus, it endorsed the rulings of the International Military Tribunal of Nuremberg, established in 1945 by the Allied Powers in the exercise of their joint control (*coimperium*) over Germany.

In accordance with the London Charter of 1945, to which the Tribunal was subject, the four Occupying Powers extended the traditional jurisdiction regarding breaches of the laws of war, that is, war crimes in the strict sense, to crimes against peace and related crimes against humanity. All this meant was that the Allies did jointly what each of them could have done and did individually regarding alleged war criminals in his hands. The endorsement of these principles by the General Assembly of the United Nations had merely the effect of estopping members of the United Nations from contesting in future the assumption by belligerents of such an extended jurisdiction.

Some further progress on traditional lines was attained, again under the auspices of the International Committee of the Red Cross, in the four Geneva Conventions of 1949 on the Protection of War Victims, and a Convention, sponsored by UNESCO on the Protection of Cultural Property in the Event of Armed Conflict (1954).

Yet, these advances on the humanitarian front were more than balanced by powerful trends towards total war.

(a) *Trends towards Total War in the Past*

In three types of war the danger of exacerbation is greater in most civilisations than in other wars: general wars, civil wars and, worst of all, ideological wars.

General wars are more likely to become wars to the finish than duel wars, with the other members of the international society as watchful onlookers. Civil wars give vent to all the bitterness of apparently insoluble family quarrels. The parties to ideological wars are prone to magnify the objectives of war into absolute postulates and reduce the enemy to a sub-human level.

The first of these types of all-out war is illustrated by the Peloponnesian War between Athens and Sparta (431-404 B.C.). The Crusades, the wars of extermination against heretics such as the Albigenses, the religious wars of the sixteenth and seventeenth century and the Spanish War (1936-39) illustrate the second and third of these types of war.

In any of these types of war, initially observed rules tend to vanish in a crescendo of increasingly ruthless reprisals and counter-reprisals. Even in more limited wars, it is tempting for a retreating army to adopt scorched-earth policies—more recently termed "area denial" to the enemy— as did the French in the German Palatinate in the late seventeenth century and the Russians in their own country during the Napoleonic Wars.

Sea warfare presents difficulties of its own. The simultaneous use of the high seas for peaceful and hostile purposes encourages countries in command of the seas to treat enemy merchant ships, especially if armed, as enemy naval ships, and neutral ships carrying contraband as enemy ships. Similarly, weak sea Powers expect to gain more than lose by hit-and-run tactics or resort to indiscriminate submarine or air warfare against shipping of any type. These methods leave little scope for avoiding unnecessary losses in enemy life, ships and cargo. Thus, in sea warfare, the tendencies towards total warfare were always more pronounced than in land warfare.

In the First World War, a contest with, as the war spread, growing ideological overtones, the trends towards total war proved irresistible. On land, flame-throwers and poison gas, and, at sea, unanchored contact mines and submarines were added to the arsenals of the belligerents. With the advent of air bombing, warfare reached into a new dimension, and, more than any long-range artillery or naval bombardment, this type of warfare contributed to blurring the distinctions between combat zones, enemy-occupied territories and the homelands of belligerents.

The pre-1939 period witnessed Italy's application of mustard gas against the bare-footed Ethiopian levies in circumstances in which the Fascist invaders had not to fear retaliation in kind. In the Second World War, the willingness of belligerents to take full advantage of any promising technological innovation grew apace.

In the form of area and carpet bombing, they paid an increasingly nominal attention to the restraining concept of the military objective, and napalm and phosphorus bombs increased the terror element in this type of warfare. This reached its culmination in the use of nuclear bombs against Hiroshima and Nagasaki.

Unlimited submarine warfare, the inhuman treatment of Eastern prisoners of war and civilians by Nazi Germany and of internees of all categories in the Japanese "co-prosperity" sphere completed a picture which had little in common with any idea of civilised warfare. In one form or another belligerents on both sides increasingly accepted the priority of military necessities and, sooner rather than later, transgressed the thin border line that separates this type of pragmatism from total warfare and neo-barbarism.

(b) *Towards Total Warfare?*

In drawing a balance-sheet of the trends in contemporary world society towards and against total war, eight pointers may be of assistance:

(1) The international quasi-order of the United Nations has too many loop-holes to outlaw war effectively as a social institution. Each of the world Powers may exercise its veto power under Chapter Seven of the Charter, so as to prevent the application of sanctions against itself.

In at least seven situations it is hardly practicable to submit to impartial verification the legal or illegal character of war under the Charter of the United Nations: wars in which a competent organ of the United Nations fails to agree in the form required by the Charter on the identification of the aggressor; wars in inaccessible border areas as in the armed encounters between India and China or China and the Soviet Union; wars with or between contending governments of divided States, some of which are not recognised by some member States of the United Nations, as in Korea and Vietnam; new types of "just" wars as, in the view of Communist and Afro-Asian States, wars against remnants of salt-water colonialism; armed interventions under the banner of limited sovereignty in the "socialist Commonwealth" of the Soviet Union and her European allies and in the "democratic" Caribbean hinterland of the United States of America; anticipatory or interceptive self-defence, as invoked by Israel in the Six-Day War of 1967; retaliatory armed strikes, as practised by

Israel in recent years, and "forward" defensive strategies, as envisaged by the NATO High Command.

(2) The totalitarian or authoritarian character of the greater number of members of the United Nations and the manner in which, even in democratic States, public opinion can be manipulated over affairs such as the Gulf of Tonkin incident (1964) are directly relevant. They make it difficult to rely on public opinion as an effective restraint of any government which has decided to condition public opinion towards escalation of an armed conflict into near-total or total warfare.

(3) The acceleration of technical "progress" makes possible not only new "families" of existing weapons of mass destruction, including nuclear cluster bombs and new forms of missile warfare, but also new types of warfare such as the creation of automated battlefields and warfare from satellites orbiting in space.

If experience is the test, leaders who know that if they lose the war they will in any case be tried and found guilty as war criminals by their enemies, will sooner or later prefer whatever, at the time, is offered to them as a decisive "miracle" weapon to ultimate defeat.

(4) The preponderance in the contemporary world of an increasing number of mass societies makes most of these liable to respond to primitive and emotive oversimplifications of an ideological character. Such quasi-religions tend to encourage the transformation of relative values into absolute goals and provide ready justifications for wars to the finish by fair means or foul.

(5) Especially in poor countries with retrograde education facilities and ruling cliques which depend on the armed forces as the most effective guarantee of some internal order, neo-barbarism in the form of a relapse into pristine tribalism tends to reduce internal war to mechanised carnage.

(6) The tendency, even in more settled communities, of large sections of uprooted urbanised elements to organise themselves in subtribal groups further stimulates pathological tendencies towards aggressiveness, terrorism and guerrilla warfare.

(7) In such an atmosphere, the propagated assimilation of internal armed conflicts to international armed conflicts is unlikely to impose civilising restraints on the conduct of civil wars. It tempts the forces of "law and order" to conduct what ought to be conceived as police operations as if they were international armed conflicts.

(8) The anonymity of the most sophisticated forms of contemporary push-button, computer, missile, chemical and biological warfare makes it even more improbable that programmers will overfeed their robots with legal and humanitarian restraints. Thus, the new mortal gods who are likely to decide on the responses in future major crises can be expected to be even more neurotic and obtuse than their predecessors.

CONCLUSIONS

Professional optimists, more frequently disproved than borne out by experience, may consider this impressionist picture to be overdrawn in dark colours. Admittedly, it is influenced by the experiences of a generation which has seen two world wars fought for grand causes with increasing ferocity, and civil wars and inter-communal slaughter on a scale outclassing the carnages of past ages.

Yet, is this evaluation of the trends in the present-day world towards a relapse into violence unlimited and neo-barbarism so far-fetched?.

International law, like any other branch of law, is an instrument of social control. It is not, and cannot be, a self-executing system which operates in a social vacuum. Whether it serves civilising processes or trends in the opposite direction depends on its subjects in the double meaning of the term.

Thus, in a strongly hierarchical world society, held together by a precarious world quasi-order, the world Powers are, in the abstract, the only effective international policemen. The relevance of others, such as United Nations *ad hoc* or permanent contingents, depends on consensus between the super-Powers. Yet, if the super-Powers are divided or, for fear of escalation of internal or local armed conflicts into international or general armed conflicts, are unwilling to restrain their own allies or satellites, or if they themselves indulge in the luxury of experiments in brinkmanship, the dykes of twentieth-century world civilisation are unlikely to be strong enough to withstand the rising tide of neo-barbarism.

This "doom-watch" style analysis of a growing imbalance between the forces sustaining and undermining international law and peace suggests that efforts towards further improving the humanitarian aspects of the law of armed conflict will continue to have but a limited use. More likely than not, they will also in future assist in diminishing the sum total of human misery. Yet, increasingly, they will tend to become fringe activities.

In the present equilibrium between the requirements of the standard of civilisation and the destructive potentialities of war, what is needed above all is a thorough readjustment of priorities of self-interest, especially among the super-Powers. This calls, in the first place, for a measure of agreement on the identification of the chief enemies of civilisation, and two of these are surely violence and chaos on any major scale anywhere in the world. Secondly, this diagnosis calls for the primary concentration of energy on shoring up the dykes of world civilisation. Otherwise, little hope exists for the survival of present world civilisation or international law as a civilising instrument. Thus, in itself, the state of the Law of Armed Conflict may be of rather limited significance. Yet, it remains a fairly accurate gauge for sensing the direction in which mankind appears to be heading.

SUGGESTIONS FOR INTER-DISCIPLINARY READING

Ardrey, R. *The Territorial Imperative* (1967)
Beeler, T. *Warfare in Feudal Europe* (1971)
Beaumont, R.A., and Martin, E. (eds.). *War in the Next Decade* (1975)
Belperron, P. *La Croisade contre les Albigeois* (1942)
Boddard, L. *Massacre on the Amazon* (1972)
Bohannan, B. (ed.). *Law and Warfare : Studies in the Anthropology of Conflict* (1967)
Bowett, D.W. *Self-Defence in International Law* (1958)
Brown, D. *Bury My Heart at Wounded Knee* (1971)
Brownlie, I. *International Law and the Use of Force by States* (1963)
Burton, J.W. *Conflict and Communication* (1969)
Carnegie Endowment for International Peace. *The Law of Armed Conflicts* (1971—including a concise Report, covering the whole subject, by Denise Bindschedler-Robert)
Calder, N. (ed.) *Unless Peace Comes: A Scientific Forecast for New Weapons* (1968)
Clark, G. *World Prehistory* (1969)
Clark, J.D. *The Prehistory of Africa* (1970)
Clarke, R. *The Science of War and Peace* (1971)
Collingwood, R.G. *The New Leviathan* (1942)
Corpus Juris Militaris (Leipzig, 1724)
Draper, G.I.A.D. *The Red Cross Conventions* (1958)
Falk, R.A. (ed.). *The Vietnam War and International Law* (3 vols.—1968-72); *The International Law of Civil War* (1971)
Fuller, T.F.C. *The Decisive Battles of the Western World and their Influence upon History* (1954)
Gardner, R., and Heider, K.G. *Gardens of War: Life and Death in the New Guinea Stone Age* (1969)
Guevara, Che. *Guerilla Warfare* (1961)
Hewitt, H.J. *The Organisation of War under Edward III, 1338-62* (1966)
Higgins, R. *United Nations Peacekeeping 1946-1967* (3 vols- 1969-);*Conflict of Interests* (1965)
International Committee of the Red Cross. *Conference of Government Experts on the Reaffirmation and Development of International Humanitarian Law Applicable in Armed Conflicts* (Second Session—2 vols.—1972)
Johnson, D.H.N. *Rights in Air Space* (1965)
Kahn,H. *On Escalation* (1965)
Kalshoven, F. *Belligerent Reprisals* (1971)
Keen, M.H. *The Laws of War in the Late Middle Ages* (1965)
Lawick-Goodall, H., and T. van.*Innocent Killers* (1970)
Lorenz, K. *Das Sogenannte Boese* (1963, translated into English by M. Latzke under the title *On Aggression,* 1966)
Luard, E. (ed.). *The International Regulation of Civil Wars* (1972)
McDougal, M.S.,and Associates. *Studies in World Public Order* (1960)
McDougal, M.S.,and Feliciano. F.P., *Law and Minimum World Public Order* (1961)
Mao Tse-Tung. *Selected Military Writings* (Peking, 1963)
Marighella, C. *Minimanual of the Urban Guerrilla* (1971)
Morris, D. *The Human Zoo* (1969)

Numelin, R. *The Beginnings of Diplomacy* (1950)
Prawdin, M. *The Mongol Empire* (1940)
Runciman, Sir Steven. *A History of the Crusades* (3 vols.: 1951-54)
St. Torre, T. de. *The Nigerian Civil War* (1972)
Schwarzenberger, G. *The Law of Armed Conflict* (1968); *International Law and Order* (1971)
Stein, E. *Impact of New Weapons Technology on International Law, Recueil,* Hague Academy of International Law, Vol. 132 (1971)
Stockholm International Peace Research Institute. *The Problem of Chemical and Biological Warfare* (6 vols.—1971-73; *Napalm and Incendiary Weapons* (1972)
Stone, J. *Aggression and World Order* (1958); *Legal Controls of International Conflict* (1959)
Sun Tzu. *The Art of War* (between 400 and 320 B.C.—translated by S.B. Griffith, 1963)
Thucydides. *History of the Peloponnesian War* (translated by B. Werner, 1972)
Toynbee, A.J. *A Study of History,* Vol. 12: Reconsiderations (1961)
United Nations. Reports of the Secretary-General on *Respect for Human Rights* (A/7720, 1969 and A/8052, 1970); Report of the Secretary-General on *Napalm and other incendiary weapons* (A/8803, October 9, 1972)

Chapter 6

EUROPEAN COMMON LAW

"....in ipso jure Gentium Europaearum, jure inquam earum communi"

John Selden, *Mare Clausum* (1636 - I, 24)

The perspective in which it is proposed to examine in this Chapter the law of the European Communities is that of European Common Law.[1]

I—MEANINGS OF COMMON LAW

Before attempting to elaborate the meanings of European Common Law, it is advisable to recall briefly the meanings of the term *Common Law* in English and Continental Law.

In the evolution of *English Law*, the term *Common Law* is primarily employed as a contrast to Equity and Statute Law. Yet it has an older and, for our purposes, more significant meaning. It also stands for the law applied in all the Kings's Courts. In this meaning, Common Law is distinguished from local law, such as the law of the manor, and the law applicable to particular transactions and groups of men, such as the law merchant.

In the history of *Continental Law*, concepts comparable to Common Law in its third meaning are expressed in terms such as *jus generale, usus generalis, droit commun* and *Gemeinrecht*.

By *jus generale*, the Glossators of the twelfth and thirteenth centuries understood the Roman Law, rediscovered in the Renaissance. They contrasted this *ratio scripta* with the multitude of local laws (*leges speciales).*

Their successors, the Commentators or Post-Glossators of the fourteenth and fifteenth centuries, viewed *lex generalis* from a more practical angle. Their *usus generalis Pandectarum* (subsequently referred to as the law of the Pandects) embodied an amalgam of Roman, Germanic and Canon Law, in the seventeenth century also termed *jurisprudentia Romano-Germanica*; *droit commun* and *Gemeinrecht* were French and German synonyms.

In theory, this Common Law was subsidiary to local law. In practice, the position was different. *Jus generale* could be made to serve more

[1] This Chapter is a continuation of experiments made under the same title in the early sixties: a lecture course at the Luxembourg *Faculté Internationale de Droit Comparé* (1961) and a lecture at the British Institute of International and Comparative Law, chaired by Lord Diplock (1962).

readily than local laws the interests of the rising class of absolutist rulers. The doctors turned out by the Law Schools of the Commentators and appointed in increasing numbers to the law courts of the new territorial rulers achieved these ends by a simple procedural device. As *usus generalis*, the law of the Pandects did not have to be proved. It was automatically applied by the courts in the absence of proof of a contradictory local law and, unless the local law happened to be written law, the courts made the burden of proving it a heavy task.

From the end of the eighteenth century onwards, absolutist rulers of the Enlightenment era created their own, if territorially limited, Common Law by way of comprehensive codifications. From the time of Napoleon onwards, the newly emerging bourgeois class employed similar techniques to clear away the remnants of ancient, local and feudal laws hampering commerce and *laissez-faire* liberalism. These codifications reduced the former Common Law of the Pandects to a shadowy existence in the Law Schools of the Continental universities.[2]

II—TYPES OF EUROPEAN COMMON LAW

Absolutism, liberalism and territorial sovereignty on the Continent made short shrift of the old Common Law. Yet, while the law of the Pandects declined, a new European Common Law emerged.

It is advisable to distinguish between at least four types of this European Common Law[3]:

European Common Law: First Type

In their relations with each other, the European territorial States had developed common usages and habits that were systematised into a coherent body of *international customary law*: the public law of Europe. This body of law may be considered as European Common Law in its first meaning.

2 For purposes of general orientation, see F.C. von Savigny, *Geschichte des Roemischen Rechts im Mittelalter* (7 vols.—1834-1851); H. Kantorowicz, *Studies in the Glossators of the Roman Law* (1938); Sir Frederick Pollock and F.W. Maitland, *The History of English Law* (1923), Vol. I, pp. 107 *et seq.*, 153 *et seq.* and 190 *et seq.*; Th. F.T. Plucknett, *A Concise History of the Common Law* (1956), Part 2; P. Koschaker, *Europa und das Roemische Recht* (1947); *Jus Commune* (*Veroeffentlichungen des Max-Planck-Instituts fuer Europaeische Rechtsgeschichte* (Frankfurt am Main, 1967-) and, for an instructive case study, K.K. Finke, *Die Tuebinger Juristenfakultaet 1477-1534* (1972).

3 For other illustrations of European Common Law on various levels of integration, see H. Mosler, 19 C.L.P. (1966), p. 168 *et seq.* See also below, note 6.

In a more comprehensive survey, it would also be necessary to pay attention to the Canon Law of the Roman Catholic Church as a distinct type of European Common Law and, from the angle of Comparative Law, to consider the legal principles common to all or most European legal systems or, at least, to those in each of the halves of a divided post-1945 Europe.

On the relevance of principles of law recognised by the members of the Communities for purposes of the fourth type of European Common Law, see below under this sub-heading.

When European society expanded into a world society, the European nations were the active agents in this process. They treated their European public law as self-evident and fair enough to be acceptable to any civilised State. In any case, this was the only assumption on which they were prepared to recognise other entities as subjects of international law, and the great Powers of Europe were strong enough to make their view prevail.

In the process of generalisation of the public law of Europe, international customary law gained universality in scope but at the price of largely losing its European and Christian ethical basis. It became formalised as a set of legal rules of an essentially jurisdictional and enabling character.

European Common Law: Second Type

The enabling rules of international customary law made possible a further type of European Common Law: legal rules and patterns of a consensual character. Excepting the great peace settlements and some other multilateral treaties, these treaties were preponderantly of a bilateral character. This *treaty law* constitutes European Common Law in its second meaning.

If, topic by topic, world maps were charted, such a world atlas of international treaty law would probably reveal a considerably more intensive network of legal relations between European States since the Napoleonic Wars than between European and non-European States. Edward Hertslet's *The Map of Europe by Treaty, showing the various political and territorial changes which have taken place since the General Peace of 1814*[4] is a pioneer work in this treatment of European Common Law.

European Common Law: Third Type

With the division of the world and Europe into eristic blocs in the post 1945 era, the first and second types of European Common Law have lost some of their former significance. Yet, in the confederate superstructures created on both sides of the dividing line between Western and Eastern Europe, new rules of consensual European law have been created in organisations such as the Council of Europe and the Council for Mutual Economic Aid (Comecon).

In territorial scope, the Western variant of post-1945 European Common Law roughly corresponds to that of Roman Law during the second century, historically the earliest—if imperial and internal—version of European Common Law. The Council of Europe law does not, however, extend to the Iberian Peninsula.

The third type of European Common Law has three distinct features.

[4] 3 vols. (1875)

First, international protection of a number of human rights by way of binding legal obligation on a multilateral footing has been achieved. *Secondly*, the interpretation and application of the 1950 European Convention on Human Rights and its supplementary Protocols by, at least optional, quasi-judicial and judicial organs has been secured.[5] *Thirdly*, a considerable number of additional multilateral conventions, primarily of a cultural character, has been initiated by the Council of Europe.[6] The subjects covered extend from legal co-operation to cultural relations, patents and television, social policy and public health.

This confederate and multilateral treaty law of Western Europe constitutes European Common Law in its third meaning.

European Common Law: Fourth Type

In a narrower belt of Western Europe, covered by the three European Communities, European Common Law has reached the highest degree of integration so far achieved.[7] Leaving aside the British Isles and the Associated States in South-East Europe and Africa, the territorial scope of the three Communities corresponds by and large to that of Charlemagne's Empire.

The differences between the Law of the European Communities and the Law of the Council of Europe are qualitative rather than quantitative. They can be summarised under five heads:

(1) *Subject-matter.* The constituent instruments of the three Communities cover activities that, in terms of power, are less peripheral than those entrusted to the Council of Europe.

(2) *Organisation.* Although the European Communities and some of their commentators do not yet appear to have recovered from the shock of the Luxembourg understandings of January 29, 1966, the Communities are probably still best understood in terms of experiments in functional federalism.[8]

(3) *Personal scope.* Access by those to whom the Court of Justice of

[5] On recent developments, see, for instance, J. Fawcett, 24 C.L.P. (1971), p. 246 *et seq.*

[6] On the status of these conventions, see the latest Chart on Signatures and Ratifications of Council of Europe Conventions, published by the Directorate of Legal Affairs of the Council of Europe.

If the thaw in the Cold War between West and East Europe should continue, scope may exist for an additional type of European Common Law. The foundations for such a truly *regional* type of European Common Law have been laid in highly specialised and technical fields by the United Nations Commission for Europe. If a greater need for more multilateral European Conventions on this scale should arise, the intensification of studies in European Comparative Law, as outlined above (note 3) would be advisable.

[7] On the meanings of international integration, see Mosler, *loc. cit.* above, note 3, p. 177, *ibid.* p. 201, and, further, *ibid.* Vol. 16, (1963), p. 22 *et seq.*

[8] See, further, below under III; 16 C.L.P. (1963), p. 17 *et seq.*, and, *contra*, I. Seidl-Hohenveldern, *ibid.* Vol. 25 (1972), p. 18 *et seq.*

the European Communities is open and who are subject to its jurisdiction, does not depend on optional concurrence, subject to potential limitations in time and scope, by each member State. This is an essential difference between the Court of Justice of the Communities and the two comparable organs of the Council of Europe, the European Commission of Human Rights and the European Court of Human Rights.

(4) *Powers of decision-making.* The wide range of secondary legislative and executive powers of the European Communities rounds off the picture of supranational institutions that, in powers of decision-making, are better endowed than typical international institutions on the confederate level such as the United Nations and its Specialised Agencies or the Council of Europe.

(5) *Quantity of consensual jus cogens.* Beginnings of a consensual *jus cogens* are noticeable in the Council of Europe in what, occasionally, the European Commission of Human Rights has termed *l'ordre public Européen.* Yet in the Council of Europe, these trends are, so far, embryonic. In the practice of the Court of Justice of the European Communities, a remarkable body of judicially interpreted and developed Common Law—termed *droit commun* or *droit de la Communauté* by the Court itself—is gradually accumulating. It includes principles of law common to the legal systems of the members of the Communities which are treated by the Court of Justice as relevant subsidiary rules.

The Law of the European Communities—in substance, a sophisticated body of International Economic Law—has six characteristics:

(1) This Common Law amounts to the emergence of an *autonomous* body of law (*corps de droit—Rechtskoerper*) which must be applied by the courts of all member States.[9]

(2) This Common Law is the product of the *transfer of substantive rights of national sovereignty* to Communities with legal personalities of their own.[10] It is also relevant that two of the three Communities have been created for an unlimited period.[11]

(3) This Common Law overrides conflicting national laws of member States (*la préeminance du droit communautaire*).[12]

9 *Costa* v. *E.N.E.L.* (case 6/64—10 *Recueil* (1964—French text), p. 1141, at p. 1160). See also *Van Gend en Loos* v. *Administration Fiscale Néerlandaise* (case 26/62)—9 *ibid.* (1963), p. 1, at pp. 23-25).

10 *Costa* v. *E.N.E.L., loc. cit.* above, note 9, p. 1159.
On the international aspects of the legal personalities of the Communities, see *Commission* v. *Council of the European Communities* (case 22/70—17 *Recueil* (1971—French text), p. 263, at p. 274).

11 In contrast to EEC and EURATOM, ECSC exists for a fixed term of fifty years.

12 *Costa* v. *E.N.E.L., loc. cit.* above, note 9, p. 1159.

(4) This Common Law necessarily requires uniform interpretation and application throughout the Communities.[13]

(5) This Common Law contains a number of *directly applicable legal rules* which need no further implementation by the Commission of the Communities nor any member State. These complete and unconditionally binding rules produce direct legal effects not only in the relations between the Communities and their member States but also in those between the member States and their own nationals, and it is the duty of national courts of member States to protect these rights.[14]

(6) This Common Law contains a number of rules which have the character of consensual *jus cogens*, that is, they are immune from contradictory agreements by any individual parties and invalidate agreements incompatible with such peremptory rules.[15]

In *Costa* v. *E.N.E.L.* (1964), the Court of Justice of the Communities explained the source of the strength of the fourth type of European Common Law. It is the solidity of its sociological basis: the reciprocal interest of the members of the Communities in the observance of this law.[16] If this mutual interest is lacking, or any one of the member States plays truant, the dissensions preceding the Luxembourg understandings of 1966 teach the, as yet, precarious character of the Community efforts. Thus, in their potentialities rather than achievements, these *experiments in functional federalism* deserve the appellation of a distinct, and fourth, type of European Common Law.

III—EUROPEAN COMMON LAW AND LEVELS OF INTERNATIONAL INTEGRATION

A single illustration, which, it is hoped, has been fairly chosen, must suffice to illustrate more concretely the impact of European integration on

13 *Hagen O.H.G.* v. *Einfuhr- und Vorratsstelle Getreide* (case 49/71—18 *Recueil* (1972), p. 23, at pp. 34-35).
See, further, Sir Geoffrey Howe, 49 *International Affairs* (1973), p. 2.

14 *Costa* v. *E.N.E.L., loc. cit.* above, note 9, p. 1167.
For illustrations of the growing list of judicially approved *lex perfecta* of Community Law, see G. Bebr, 19 I.C.L.Q. (1970), p. 257 *et seq.*, and P.S. Mathijsen, *A Guide to European Community Law* (1975), pp. 5-6.
On the varying scope of the direct applicability of these rules "in accordance with the Treaties" (s. 2 (1) of the European Communities Act 1972), see, for instance Arts. 177, 187 and 192 of the EEC Treaty, and, further, Sir Geoffrey Howe, *loc. cit.* above, note 13, p. 4 *et seq.*

15 *Muellers* v. *Economic and Social Committee of EEC and EURATOM* (case 79/70—17 *Recueil* (1971), p. 689, at p. 698).

16 *Costa* v. *E.N.E.L., loc. cit.* above, note 9, p. 1159
See also the perceptive study by B. Simma, *Das Reziprozitaetselement im Zustandekommen voelkerrechtlicher Vertrage* (1972), pp. 61, 73 and 83 *et seq.*

specific rules of international law and European Common Law.

The issue selected is a political postulate that, on various levels of international law and organisation, has struggled for legal expression and recognition for over a quarter of a century: the principle of equal remuneration of men and women for equal work.

United Nations Law

In international *customary* law, the question of equal remuneration of men and women is in the exclusive jurisdiction of every subject of international law.

In the Charter of the *United Nations*, the principle is covered, at least implicitly, by the enumeration among the objectives of the United Nations of the wider principle of the "equal rights of men and women" and the elaboration of these objectives in Article 1 of the Charter under the heading of promotion and encouragement of respect for human rights and fundamental freedoms for all without distinction, among others, as to sex.

These objectives are repeated in Article 55 of the United Nations Charter and underlined by the pledge of member States, contained in Article 56, to take joint and separate action in co-operation with the United Nations for the achievement of these purposes.

At most, the undertakings embodied in the Charter of the United Nations are *pacta de contrahendo* regarding the realisation of the objectives outlined above. Yet they do not constitute legal obligations to take any particular action on national or international levels.

In Article 23 (2) of the Universal Declaration of Human Rights of 1948, the principle is stated without qualification or exception: "Everyone, without any discrimination, has the right to equal pay for equal work." The "right" is, however, a merely moral, and not a legal, right.

The same is true of the 1967 Declaration of the United Nations General Assembly on Elimination of Discrimination against Women and Article 15 of the Proclamation of Tehran, 1968, adopted by a United Nations Conference on Human Rights.

The reasons advanced for these postulates in the 1967 Declaration and the 1968 Proclamation assist in understanding the political and social ideologies behind these articles of faith and belief, as they are termed in these documents: the need to eliminate all forms of discrimination, the fundamental injustice of discrimination against women, the incompatibility of such discrimination with human dignity and the welfare of the family and society, and the elimination of any form of discrimination against women as a necessity for the progress of mankind.

Potential standard-setting effects on international and national levels apart, these para-legal instruments may have one limited legal effect even on the universalist level of the United Nations. If adopted unanimously or with near-unanimity, they may be thought to create estoppels against assertions of the lawfulness of rules and practices to the contrary by members of the United Nations who have voted in their favour or by future members who join the United Nations in awareness of the existence of these standards.

In the International Covenant on Economic, Social and Cultural Rights of December 16, 1966, an attempt was made to translate these moral precepts into legal obligations. The Parties to the Covenant guarantee that the rights enunciated in the Covenant will be exercised without discrimination of any kind, for instance as to sex (Article 2 (2)), and they affirm the equal rights of men and women to the enjoyment of all the rights enumerated in the Covenant (Article 3).

More specifically, the right of enjoyment of just and favourable conditions of work is to include fair wages and "equal remuneration for work of equal value without distinction of any kind, in particular women being guaranteed conditions of work not inferior to those enjoyed by men, with equal pay for equal work" (Article 7 (*a*)(I)).

Since January 3, 1976, the Covenant is in force. The European States which have ratified or acceded to the Covenant are Bulgaria, Byelorussian SSR, Cyprus, Czechoslovakia, Denmark, Federal Republic of Germany, Finland, German Democratic Republic, Hungary, Norway, Romania, Sweden, Ukrainian SSR, USSR and Yugoslavia.

International Labour Law

In the 1919 Constitution of the *International Labour Organisation* (*ILO*) the rule of equal remuneration of men and women for work of equal value constituted one of the principles that the Parties to the Peace Treaties of 1919-20 considered to be of special and urgent importance (Article 427 of the Peace Treaty of Versailles of 1919).

In the Philadelphia Declaration of 1944, incorporated in the revised ILO Constitution of 1946, the right of all human beings, irrespective of, for instance, sex, is affirmed to pursue their material well-being and spiritual development in conditions of, among others, equal opportunity. Similarly, the principle of "equal remuneration for work of equal value" is included in the preamble of the revised ILO Constitution.

In the International Labour Convention No. 100 of June 29, 1951, an attempt has been made to create some legal obligations for Contracting Parties to put into effect on the national level the principle of equal remuneration of men and women for work of equal value. The Convention is a masterpiece of drafting in fourteen Articles of what, in post-1945 ILO parlance, has become known as a "policy and promotional" rather than a "strict obligation convention."

By January 1, 1976, the Convention had received eighty-seven ratifications. Twenty-nine of the parties are European States, including all the members of the European Communities and all the Comecon countries. The United States of America is a prominent non-party.

The Convention is supplemented by the Equal Remuneration Recommendation, 1951, which gives guidance on ways of implementing the Convention by legislation or otherwise if any Contracting Party should be so inclined.

Another International Labour Convention of similar elasticity which, by implication, covers non-discrimination between the sexes—the International Labour Convention and Recommendation of 1958 on Discrimination (Employment and Occupation)—has also been ratified by eighty-seven States (January 1, 1976). They include twenty-three European States, five of which are members or associates of the European Communities.

Similarly, the International Labour Social Policy (Basic Aims and Standards) Convention of 1962 is of marginal relevance in this context.

Council of Europe Law

Under the aegis of the Council of Europe, the principle of equal pay for equal work is embodied in the European Social Charter of 1961, but not in the 1950 European Convention on Human Rights or any of its Protocols.

Thus, the "right of men and women workers to equal pay for work of equal value" (Article 4 (3) of the Social Charter) is not under the potential control of the European Commission of Human Rights nor the European Court of Human Rights. Moreover, the principle is not included among those of common social policy, to be pursued by all appropriate national and international means (Part I of the Social Charter), but relegated to one of the optional rules assembled in Part II of the Social Charter (Article 20 (*a*)).

Regarding accepted provisions in Part II, the Contracting Parties are bound to report, at two-yearly intervals, on the implementation of these obligations and, in case of non-acceptance, they are bound, at appropriate intervals, if and when requested by the Committee of Ministers, to report on the position (Articles 21 and 22).

The European Social Charter is in force between eleven members of the Council of Europe, including six members of the European Communities (Denmark, France, Germany, Ireland, Italy and the United Kingdom).

European Community Law

In Article 119 of the EEC Treaty it is categorically provided that "each Member State shall during the first stage ensure and subsequently maintain the application of the principle that men and women should receive equal pay for equal work."

Equal remuneration without discrimination between the sexes is further defined as, for work at piece rates, being calculated on the basis of the same unit of measurement and, for work at time rates, as "the same for the same job." The formulation of equal work, instead of equivalent work as in the ILO Convention of 1951, is intentional. It is to avoid the ambiguities resulting from the application of the test of equivalence.

It was probably not the intention of the Contracting Parties to limit Article 119 to manual workers. Thus, in the absence of an express exception as is contained in Article 48 (4) of the EEC Treaty, Article 119 applies also to the public services of the member States and the staff of the European Communities.

The EEC Treaty came into force on January 1, 1958. Thus, by January 1, 1962 (Article 8), full compliance by all member States with the principle of equal remuneration for equal work was due. Actually, on December 30, 1961, the Conference of representatives of the governments of the member States—not envisaged by the Treaty, but a convenient formula for the Council of the Community whenever it acts contrary to the intentions of the Contracting Parties at the times of the conclusion of the constituting instruments—adopted a resolution, postponing the dead-line until December 21, 1964. By June 30, 1962, any difference exceeding 15 per cent was to be reduced to 15 per cent; by June 30, 1963, any difference exceeding 10 per cent was to be reduced to 10 per cent, and by December, 1964, "all discrimination" regarding remuneration between the sexes was "to be abolished."[17]

Actually, as late as 1966, the differential of wages of men and women in the member States of the Community varied between 24.8 per cent (Italy) and 45.5 per cent (Luxembourg).[18]

Although embarrassed by uncomfortable reports of the Commission and reminders in the European Parliament,[19] the member States decided to make haste slowly with the implementation of Article 119 of the EEC

17 *EEC Bulletin* 1962, No. 1, p. 8.

On European social law and policy, see also L.-E. Trodet, *Eléments du droit social européen* (1963); E.D. Brown, 16 *Current Legal Problems* (1963), p. 178 *et seq.*, and 3 *Common Market L.R.* (1965-66), p. 184 *et seq.*, and D. Collins, 5 *J. Common Market Studies* (1966-67), No. 1, pp. 36-38.

18 I.L.O. *Report on Equal Pay for Equal Work,* November 11, 1971 (U.N. Doc. E/CN6/1550). See, further, the Report by Mme. E. Sullerot, commissioned by the Commission of the European Communities, and the comments on the Report in *The Economist* (London), January 27, 1973, p. 50.

On the complex reasons for French pressure regarding the implementation of Art. 119 of EEC Treaty, which had been incorporated in the Treaty on French initiative, see D. Swann, *The Economics of the Common Market* (1972), pp. 139-140.

See also the United Kingdom Equal Pay Act 1970 (c. 41), and S. Puddefoot, *Can We Make Equal Pay Work? The Times* (London), January 17, 1973.

19 See, for instance, the *General Reports of the EEC Commission, 1961-62,* pp. 185-186, and *1966-67*, p. 251; the *First General Report, 1967,* of the three Communities, pp. 259 and 260, and *Débats du Parlement européen,* June 15-18, 1970.

See also Art. 8 (6) and (7), EEC Treaty.

Treaty, the only Article in the Chapter on Social Policy which contains mandatory duties of member States.

This behaviour does not differ substantially from that of parties to treaties in unorganised international society or international society organised on a confederate level and, normally, individuals adversely affected cannot press on either of these levels for any remedy against the will of their home States.

By contrast, the Court of Justice of the European Communities had two opportunities of insisting on the application of Article 119 of the EEC Treaty as a complete and unconditional rule of Community Common Law.

In *Defrenne* v. *Belgium* (case 80/70),[20] the Court of Justice was requested by the Belgian Conseil d'Etat, under Article 177 of the EEC Treaty, to answer three questions: *First*, did old-age pensions, payable under statute-based social insurance schemes and financed by contributions from the State, employers and employees, constitute remuneration paid indirectly by employers to the employees under their service contracts? *Secondly*, was it lawful, in such social insurance schemes, to create different age-limits for men and women? *Thirdly*, was it correct to assume that flight stewards and stewardesses of Sabena—the employer involved—were doing the same work?

The Court held that even if there were discrimination between men and women under the social insurance schemes at issue, these schemes did not form part of the remuneration under the service contracts of the parties as required by Article 119 of the EEC Treaty. Thus there was no need for the Court to answer the second and third questions put to it. The Court used the opportunity, however, to establish that, under Article 119, the member States were bound to ensure the application of the principle of equal remuneration for equal work by men and women.[21]

In *Bauduin* (*épouse Chollet*) v. *Commission of the European Communities* (case 32/71),[22] the Court established even more clearly the complete and unconditional character of Article 119 of the EEC Treaty.

In 1962, the plaintiff, a woman of French nationality, had become a member of the staff of the Commission of the European Communities. Prior to her marriage, she never had Belgian nationality. During a period of five years preceding her appointment, she did not live regularly in Belgium nor had she ever been employed there. Thus, under the Personnel

20 17 *Recueil* (1971), p. 445 *et seq.*

21 *Ibid.* p. 451.

22 18 *Recueil* (1972), p. 363 *et seq*
See also the Court's Judgment in *Goeth-Van der Schueren,* 19 *ibid.* (1973), p. 181 *et seq.*
On the comparable Judgment by the United Nations Administrative Tribunal in *Mullan* v. *U.N. Secretary-General* (1972 – AT/DEC/162), see the writer's *International Law as Applied by International Courts and Tribunals,* Vol. III: *International Constitutional Law* (1976), p. 413 *et seq.*

Statute,[23] she was entitled to an expatriation allowance. In 1970, she married a Belgian national, who was resident in Belgium but not employed by the Communities. Because the plaintiff was married to a person residing in Belgium, the Commission of the Communities decided that she had lost her expatriation allowance. The plaintiff asked for a declaration that she continued to be entitled to receive this allowance. She also asked for the annulment of two decisions of the Commission, denying her primary request.

The Commission's refusal had been based on the Personnel Statute.[24] According to the Statute, a member of the personnel loses the right to an expatriation allowance if, in marrying a person who, at the time of the marriage, is not entitled to it, he will not acquire the status of a head of family. Moreover, it was expressly stated in the Personnel Statute that, normally, the head of the family was the married employee of male sex and, only exceptionally, as, for instance, in cases of serious illness or incapacity of the male spouse, could the female married employee be considered as the head of family.

In the plaintiff's submission, this provision amounted to a flagrant discrimination between male and female personnel of the Communities. Thus, among other legal rules invoked, it was contrary to Article 119 of the EEC Treaty and null and void.

As in the *Defrenne* case, the plaintiff argued that remuneration in the meaning of Article 119 included indirect benefits such as the expatriation allowance. As distinct from the *Defrenne* case, the Court accepted that this particular benefit was based on the service contract between the parties.

The Court held further that the provision attacked by the plaintiff amounted to an "effective" and "arbitrary" discrimination between male and female employees of the Communities. Relying expressly on Article 119 of the EEC Treaty, the Court exercised its powers of annulment under Articles 173 and 184 of the EEC Treaty and annulled the two decisions of the Commission.

In both cases, the Court of Justice of the Communities established the character of Article 119 of the EEC Treaty as a complete and unconditional legal rule. In the field of social policy that, from the point of view of hard law, is one of the least promising in the law of the three Communities, the Court made it clear to the organs of the Communities and the member States alike that this law was meant to be obeyed.

So long as the Court continues to fulfil so effectively its appointed function in the Communities—and it should be added, in the *Bauduin* case

[23] Art. 69 of the Personnel Statute and Art. 4 (1) (*a*) of Annex VII to the Personnel Statute. For the corresponding provisions in the consolidated version, in force since March 5, 1972, see *J.O. des Communautés européennes*, Vol. 15 (C 100, September 28, 1972 (French ed.), pp. 20 and 44-45.

[24] Art. 4 (3) of Annex VII.

against the advice of the Court's Advocate-General—the dynamics of the law of the Communities are far from being exhausted, and the experiments with European Common Law on the level of functional federalism may be considered as being, as yet, in progress.

CONCLUSIONS

It remains to relate to one another the various concepts and illustrations discussed in this Chapter.

The explanation of the differences between the notions of Common Law, *droit commun, Gemeinrecht,* on the one hand, and, on the other, the first three variants of European Common Law lies in the differences between the factual orders behind these bodies of law.[25]

From the angle of the relations between law and order, the essential feature of the English Common Law in the evolution of early English Law is not its relation to Equity and Statute law but the fact that this law was applied in all the King's courts and that, if required, these courts had the whole of the centralised royal power behind them. In this perspective, medieval English Common Law is more akin to the earliest type of European Common Law—Roman Law as applied at the height of the Roman Empire in most parts of the British Isles—than to *droit commun* or *Gemeinrecht* as subsequently understood in France and Germany.

It was only when the law of the Pandects became a pliable instrument of absolutist rulers that it received the vigour any mere *ratio scripta* is lacking. Yet the price of this link with territorial sovereignty was the subjection of the law of the Pandects to the exigencies of absolutist reason of State and loss of its claim to territorially unlimited validity.

The basic difference between these forms of Common Law and the first three types of European Common Law is the lack of an international order behind these types of European Law that is comparable to the orders behind English Common Law, imperial Roman law or the territorially applied law of the Pandects.

In this respect, the international law of unorganised international society and the international law of confederate institutions such as the United Nations, the International Labour Organisation and the Council of Europe are much alike. They all have to rely on precarious international quasi-orders.

The manner in which, to choose but one illustration, the members of the Council of the European Communities attempted to circumvent their obligations under Article 119 of the EEC Treaty[26] may suggest that, in this respect, any difference between international and supranational institutions is, at most, marginal. Yet, the way in which the Court of Justice of

[25] See, further, the writer's *International Law and Order* (1971), p. 5 *et seq.*

[26] See above under III.

the European Communities reasserted the common law of the Communities demonstrates that, in cases of this type, substantial differences exist between European Common Law on the confederate level and that of functional federalism.

The Common Law of the European Communities has supremacy over the national laws of the members of the Communities. The Court of Justice of the Communities lacks, however, a general jurisdiction, comparable to that of municipal courts. Thus, it was only in two types of case—invocation of the jurisdiction of the Court of Justice by a national court and action by a member of the staff of the Communities—that the issue of the complete and unconditional character of Article 119 of the EEC Treaty could be thrashed out before the Court of Justice of the Communities.

In this fourth and most advanced meaning, European Common Law may be, so far, more an aspiration than a reality. It is, however, an aspiration that, demonstrably, is in the process of being transformed into reality.

Chapter 7

CIVITAS MAXIMA?

"Therefore I cannot refrain from speaking about the city of this world, a city which aims at dominion, which holds nations in enslavement, but is itself dominated by that very lust of domination". Augustinus, *The City of God against the Pagans* (Bk I, Preface - about 414 A.D.

I—ATTEMPT AT AN EMPIRICAL SYNTHESIS

Research tends towards synthesis. Thus it is the primary object of this Chapter to attempt once again to explore the relations between world society, world law and world order and examine whether the results of more recent inter-disciplinary studies confirm earlier inquiries[1] or lead to new insights.

Moreover, since these earlier efforts, I have experimented with further techniques, such as the historical models of international law and the distinction between international law and international order. The time has now come to test the potential relevance of these tools for purposes of a synthesis of world affairs.

It is a by-product of such an empirical synopsis as is here attempted that it makes possible a critical analysis of more speculative—or intuitive—overall evaluations of international relations. Without adequate evidence, they can command no more acceptance than any other non-proven hypothesis. These *a priori* notions find their most extreme formulation in Christian von Wolff's tempting concept of *Civitas Maxima* and ethical postulates derived from it, such as the fundamental norm of international law proposed by Hersch Lauterpacht: *Voluntas civitatis maximae est servanda* (Let the will of the world community be done).

This critical function of the Chapter determines the title. The question mark emphasises that the—at least on the surface—rapidly changing character of our world environment calls for renewed analysis.

II—SOCIETY AND COMMUNITY MODELS

In spite of unavoidable possibilities of abuse, the distinction between *community* and *society* offers a useful starting point for inter-disciplinary studies in the field of international relations.

[1] See, for instance, *The Misery and Grandeur of International Law* (University College London, 1963) or *The Inductive Approach to International Law* (1964), p. 165 *et seq.*

As with other "pure" types of conceptual models, social reality does not know of any groups which wholly represent the extremes of an undiluted society or a pure community (in the former, relations based entirely on fear; in the latter, relations based entirely on love.) All existing groups occupy positions intermediate between these two poles.

In the last resort, the distinction between society and community is based on different but typical patterns of behaviour of those involved. It is difficult to examine directly the reasons for anybody's behaviour. Thus, it is advisable to subject such motives to a test that makes possible an, at least relatively, objective verification and may claim respectable theological authority: "For the tree is known by his fruit" (Matthew 12: 33). The consequences of actions and omissions are better guides to the society and community character of particular groups than unavoidably complex motives.

The differences between the two types of social relations are not absolute but relative. Awareness of the relativity of the difference between societies and communities leads to a further insight; a society can be transformed into a community, and the process can be reversed. Yet freedom of choice in either direction is limited, and possibilities vary from group to group and from one historical situation to another. Moreover, any person or group may be simultaneously involved in relations in either category.

The distinction between society and community is as fundamental for international relations as for any other branch of social studies. It facilitates the understanding of international relations as relations in concrete social environments. It provides models which are as relevant for the study of international law as of national law. It leads to a relativist approach to problems of international planning and permits a critical analysis of "committed" proposals for the improvement of world affairs.

Consciousness of the limited but always open choice between the organisation of international relations on a society or community basis has also another beneficial effect. It makes possible a sharp distinction between the treatment of the material chosen in this Chapter and "realist" analyses such as Kautilya's *Arthasastra,* Macchiavelli's *Il Principe* and Hilter's *Mein Kampf.*

III—WORLD COMMUNITY?

International relations of the past and present may differ in some respects. Yet they have one feature in common: the pivotal position of power.

The place of power is half-way between influence and force. Influence is exercised by persuasion. Force means physically enforced subordination of another's will. In contrast to influence and force, power involves the imposition of one's own will on a group or the will of one group on another, if possible without, but, if it cannot be helped, by the application of the minimum of necessary force.

On the basis of overwhelming historical material, it appears appropriate—until the contrary is proved— to understand international relations primarily as society relations and present them as, in essence, systems of open power politics or power politics in disguise.

The multitude of consecutive and overlapping international societies throughout the centuries has three characteristic features in common. The members of such international societies tend to regard their own groups as ends in themselves, and not merely as means to higher and overriding community ends. In the last resort, they consider themselves entitled to defend their existence by all means, including force. The hierarchy between the members of these societies is determined by their power, that is, ultimately, their relative strength in terms of political, economic or military conflict. These basic motivations lead to typical patterns of behaviour: self-defence (if not self-aggrandisement) as the first duty of the State; alliances; counter-alliances; balance of power systems; neutralisation; neutrality and armed conflict. In such an environment, morality and law may exist but play a merely subordinate role.

The international societies of the pre- and post-1815 periods differ in two respects: the latter are world societies and are, at least, partly organised.

Contemporary world society is the result of a threefold process: *disintegration* of the European Christian community (with all necessary reservations regarding States in which the greater part of the population were little more than serfs), *expansion* of this European society since the sixteenth century into a world society during the periods of colonialism and imperialism, and *concentration* of power in a decreasing number of great and world Powers.

From the middle of the nineteenth century onwards, this unorganised international society was transformed under the influence of liberalist, pacifist and nationalist movements. It became a partly-organised international society, endowed with weak administrative international unions and *ad hoc* arbitration tribunals.

The First World War led to renewed attempts to develop the pre-war system of open power politics into an organised community. The goal of a true world community was to be reached by the outlawry of war, disarmament, collective security, the pacific settlement of international disputes and orderly revision of dated or unjust international engagements. The Russian October Revolution of 1917 and the danger of Communist revolts in other countries suggested an additional international experiment in the administration of anodyne: the creation of an International Labour Organisation with distinct representation of employers' and workers' unions in national delegations.

The League of Nations failed to achieve the object of even relative universality, that is, an expansion of its membership to all States whose membership would have been indispensable for the successful achievement of its programme. At every critical point, decisive great and middle Powers remained outside or ceased to be members. Thus it was convenient, if superficial, to explain the failure of the League of Nations by its non-universality. It required the repetition of the League experiment in circumstances in which, from the outset, the world organisation of the United Nations had attained relative universality, to reveal the inadequacy of this analysis.

It then became evident that the reasons for the failures of both Organisations in the spheres that matter most—prevention of international armed conflicts and maintenance of world peace—were more fundamental than the non-attainment of universality.

The precarious equilibrium between the world Powers which exists at present—in spite of an increasing number of small wars and internal armed conflicts that tend to spill over into international confrontations—rests on foundations other than the seven Principles "enshrined" in Article 2 of the United Nations Charter (sovereign equality; good faith; the pacific settlement of international disputes; prohibition of the threat and use of force; collective action; extension of these Principles of the Charter of the United Nations to non-members in the interest of international peace and security, and prohibition, in principle, of United Nations intervention in matters essentially within the domestic jurisdiction of any State).

IV—WORLD LAW?

The distinction between society and community yields three models of law: the law of a society which, as, for example, in the basic regulation of property rights, serves the interests of ruling persons or groups (*Law of Power)*; the law of a community which, as, for instance, the canon law of the Roman Catholic Church, serves the interests of the group as a whole and primarily fulfils the function of rationalising generally accepted patterns of behaviour *(Law of Co-ordination),* and the law of hybrids between societies and communities which, as, for instance, the Roman or English law of contract, is based on formal or substantive reciprocity *(Law of Reciprocity).*

It contributes to the understanding not only of International Law but also of its social environment to examine this legal system in its sociological, historical and ethical perspectives.

International Law in Sociological Perspective

The inductively verifiable rules of international *customary* law can be reduced to seven legal principles: Sovereignty, Recognition, Consent,

Good Faith, Freedom of the Seas, International Responsibility, and Self-Defence. The criterion for selecting these legal principles is negative and hypothetical. If one or more of the potentially relevant groups of legal rules were excluded from such a presentation of international law, would this still permit international customary law to be fairly represented?

In the abstract, an international legal system based on rules under the above seven heads would be compatible with both an international society and an international community.

In an international *community,* such a legal system would tend to work almost automatically. The absence of a procedure for the impartial determination of the law in case of conflict could be compensated for by the willingness of those subject to the law to obey it. Given this basic attitude, there would be hardly any need for an independent procedure for the enforcement of the law. Similarly, changes in the law could be attained with the consent of all concerned.

In an international *society*, such a legal system would restrict but little the freedom of action of the players. Armaments, alliances, agreed neutralisations of territories in dispute, the acquisition of territory by cession, the creation of international protectorates and other relations of dependence, unilateral incorporation of countries not recognised as subjects of international law, and resort to force in case of real or alleged self-defence would be possible within, and despite, the existence of such a legal system.

In fields which are peripheral from the point of view of power politics, it is possible to establish legal relations of a primarily consensual character on the basis of formal or substantive reciprocity. Diplomatic relations or co-operation in the spheres of economics and communication illustrate this point. In such relations it is also possible to sublimate sanctions of power into mutual interest in the fulfilment of one's own legal obligations.

By and large, this description of a society type of international law is probably a correct sketch of international law during the period between the Napoleonic Wars and the First World War. For the sake of completeness, it would be necessary to supplement the description by reference to the partial organisation of this international society through optional international institutions. Administrative international unions and the list of arbitrators of the Permanent Court of Arbitration, which is neither permanent nor a Court, belong to this category.

In the League of Nations and the United Nations with its Specialised Agencies, this partly-organised international society was transformed into organised world societies within the frameworks of loose world confederations. This was done in ways which permitted and permit all participants, with little hindrance, to continue the game of power politics.

At first sight, decolonisation and admission to the United Nations as "sovereign and equal" States of a multitude of politically and economically unstable and militarily, at most, marginally relevant States appear to be notable counter-tendencies. They seem to point to a basic transformation of organised world society into an organised world community. Actually, these apparently novel features are probably more symptomatic of another change: the decline of salt-water empires in favour of geographically contiguous macro-political and macro-economic systems such as the United States of America, the Soviet Union, China, and, possibly, Western Europe, and of the atomisation of power in the areas between these centres of power.

In subordinate fields, systems of power politics in disguise entail changes in the superstructures of existing world society. Decisions against one of the world Powers or middle Powers by verbose majorities in organs such as the General Assembly and the Security Council of the United Nations—not to speak of the United Nations Conference on Trade and Development—are part of the game and are normally accepted by the losers with more or less good grace.

On this basis, it is also possible to pass off community versions of international morality as, for instance, the principle of national self-determination as a moral and legal principle of the organised world "community." By repetition of such claims in a mounting heap of resolutions, it may even be attempted to describe such postulates as a dynamically developing law of the United Nations.

If needs be, it is simple enough to switch back from such consensual arrangements to the level of power politics without any disguise. In matters other than those of a purely internal, and especially organisational, character, most of these international organisations are limited to the task of making recommendations. They are not allowed to make binding decisions.

In cases in which, for example, under Chapter Seven of the Charter of the United Nations, organs such as the Security Council are competent to make binding decisions, the world and great Powers of 1945 have safeguarded themselves by the reserve right of an absolute veto against unacceptable majority decisions. Similarly, they control at least negatively the admission and expulsion of member States, the election of the Secretary-General and alterations in the Charter of the United Nations.

With few exceptions such as the functional representation of employers and workers and the freedom of voting of delegates in the International Labour Organisation, delegates in the organs of the United Nations and its Specialised Agencies are government representatives in the strict sense. Thus, normally, neither the United Nations nor its Specialised Agencies may establish official contacts, without permission from the central governments of member States, with subordinate governmental or administrative organs of such States, nor give instructions to individuals in member States. In these ways, the confederate world societies established since the First World War distinguish themselves from federations, which represent the weakest form of central government in the accepted meaning of the term.

The age of decolonisation and anti-imperialism favours also other significant types and legal forms of power politics in disguise. The techniques of hegemony, that is, the guidance of equals in law by leading Powers—first described by Thucydides—are refined in confederations of the League of Nations and United Nations type. Yet they are hardly less real than in systems of open power politics. Spheres of influence of the world Powers replace direct colonial control. Association agreements, such as those of the European Economic Community with the Mediterranean and African hinterland of the European Economic Community, are the West European variants of attempts to create macro-economic preference areas which are comparable to the internal markets of the United States of America, the Soviet Union and China.

Finally, it is necessary to recall the right of withdrawal from these confederate organisations and escape clauses in their constitutions, such as Article 51 of the United Nations Charter. Under this Article, members remain entitled to take all measures they consider necessary for purposes of self-defence or collective defence against armed attack. Provisionally, each member State itself decides on what falls under this rubric and may continue with its unilateral action until the Security Council finds otherwise. If a decision under Chapter Seven of the Charter of the United Nations concerns a permanent member of the Security Council, such a State need not abstain from voting but may itself veto the decision. If it does not belong to the exclusive category of permanent members of the United Nations, it has to rely on a friendly or hegemonial Power in this most favoured class.

On a world scale, the international law of power politics in disguise distinguishes itself from the international law of open power politics less by its greater efficiency than by the additional opportunities it offers for ideological abuses. Conventions such as the Genocide Convention of 1948, the Convention of 1965 on the Elimination of all Racial Discrimination and the United Nations Covenants of 1966 on Civil and Political Rights and on Economic, Social and Cultural Rights are model illustrations of conventions which in many words say remarkably little. Even in relation to Contracting Parties, the exceptions and reservations are more important than the principles embodied in these conventions.

International Law in Historical Perspective

World history offers an abundance of material which suggests the interpretation of international relations as society relations and the classification of their correlated systems of international law in terms of society law. Conversely, any attempt to present such relations in terms of community relations and community law would be difficult to justify.

The basic historical hypotheses of these systems of international law are of dramatic and traumatic simplicity: non-peace as the normal state of affairs, rightlessness of foreigners and anarchy on the high seas. From these inauspicious beginnings developed the systems of international law of the past and present.

It makes little difference whether one investigates the international relations in the eastern Mediterranean at the times of Ramesses II or the compilation of the Old Testament; in East Asia, Europe and Asia Minor at the time of the Roman-Carthaginian rivalry, the Persian-Byzantine co-existence, the Christian-Islamic confrontation or any subsequent period. At any of these times, relations were governed decisively by power politics, with occasional excursions into power politics in disguise as with the Treaty of Eternal Peace and Alliance between Ramesses II of Egypt and King Hattušiliš III of Hatti (1270—1269 B.C.) or the Treaties of Eternal Peace of 532 and 562 A.D. between the Byzantine and Persian Empires.

The relevant international law material confirms the working hypothesis of international law as, predominantly, a law of power and reciprocity in such systems of power politics. It also reflects clearly the society character of its political environment.

There is little evidence in practice of continuity between the international law of Antiquity and the present. It is, however, true that, with remarkable consistency, power politicians have again and again relied on models of international law that have altered but little in essentials during three millennia.[2]

International Law in Ethical Perspective

Already Plato explained the need for the existence of law side by side with morality. Only if all of us were prepared at all times to do everything we recognised to be right, would the need cease for law, in addition to morality.

What is "right" depends more on the social environment of morality and law than on either of these normative systems. There are society ethics, such as Spinoza's proposition of *homo homini lupus* in an unorganised society, and community ethics, such as Christian von Wolff's postulate of the weal of the community as the supreme "law" of his *civitas maxima.*

In the form of the minimum standards of civilisation, pre-1914 international customary law incorporated such community values in three fields: the limitation of recognition in State practice to candidates which recognising States, rightly or wrongly, regarded as being civilised; a minimum standard, observance of which, at least in relation to foreign nationals, could be expected from civilised States, and the laws of war applicable between civilised States.

In Article 38 of the Statute of the Permanent Court of International Jus-

[2] See, further, above, Chapter 3, Section II.

tice of the League of Nations and the International Court of Justice of the United Nations, the general principles of law recognised by civilised nations are enumerated—after international treaties and general international customary law—as the third of the law-creating processes of contemporary international law.

It is legitimate to introduce norms of society or community ethics into international law by one of the three above-mentioned law-creating processes. Thus, for instance, the rules governing the principle of good faith in the meaning of *jus aequum* have been received into international customary law.

Attempts to smuggle rules of any system of morality into international law irrespective of such transformation constitute pretensions which must be rejected. If such alleged rules of pseudo-international law fulfil the function of supporting an existing *status quo,* they are typical illustrations of a conservative natural law. In the reverse case, they fulfil corresponding functions of a revolutionary natural law.

In all cases in which the reception of ethical norms by international law cannot be inductively verified, such meta-legal norms remain what they are: self-cancelling postulates of society and community morality or self-neutralising natural-law ideologies and utopias.

In this context, the term "Common Law of Mankind" also deserves attention. By addressing the human substratum of national and international groups at large, proponents of this concept are able to skirt round any analysis of the actual international environment in which this Common Law is supposed to apply. Moreover, whenever it suits them, they can argue that this environment is, or ought to be, viewed as an international community in the technical sense. It then takes but one further step to indulge in any natural-law phantasies that, according to personal predilection, may be termed creative, imaginative or, perhaps more accurately, speculative or messianic.

V—WORLD ORDER?

The need for the distinction between law and order can be readily demonstrated by reference to the conquest pattern of the rise of the territorial State.

If an armed group establishes itself in a country and subjects the local population to its sway, such an order of force may dispense with law altogether. The conquerors may, however, prefer to organise the territory in question by means of schools, churches, administrative services and judicial institutions.

In such cases, as for example, the Norman conquest of England or the establishment of a colonial regime overland or overseas, the law serves primarily the interests of the conquerors. If necessary, this law of power receives the requisite support from the background apparatus of overwhelming physical force in the shape of police forces, militias and armed services.

Analogous situations exist in totalitarian and authoritarian legal systems in relation to suppressed or outlawed groups. The treatment of Jews, gypsies or other "sub-human" beings in the Third Reich illustrates this proposition.

The more a legal system falls into the category of community law, the less need exists for the distinction between law and the factual order sustaining it. It may even happen that this factual order is fully integrated in the community law and subject to its control.

In other words, the more a legal system has the character of a society law, the more apparent are the functions of the dualism of order and law. There is a good reason for this. A law of power enjoys greater social prestige than a mere order of force. Without decisively altering the substance of such an order, the law of power contributes to at least some legitimation of the factual order of force that supports it.

In international societies based on power, territorial States have proved themselves to be the strongest units. By mutual recognition as sovereign States, these associations create for their own benefit normative legitimations of their monopolistic claims inside their territories. By co-operation with each other, they can control more effectively than would otherwise be possible horizontal cross-sections of an economic character, such as international and multinational companies, and secure their territorial supremacy against such intruders and competitors.

The international *de facto* order of a system of open power politics is as precarious or stable as the equilibrium between the major Powers of any age. Yet, so far, any system of open power politics has ended in a major war. Thus these systems are less orders of peace than inter-war orders. It is therefore more accurate to describe them as international quasi-orders, rather than international orders with implied claims to an effectiveness they evidently lack.

The League of Nations period of world power politics in disguise proved that, in this respect, the confederate world society of the period between the First and Second World Wars differed but little from the preceding inter-war periods.

Bearing in mind the structural similarities between the League of Nations and the United Nations, and the experiences gained with the United Nations in action, it is advisable, until convincing proof to the contrary is furnished, to view also this confederate super-structure as merely an international quasi-order. It is precariously poised on the ever-changing equilibrium between the nuclear Powers, that is, the "overkill" capacity of two—and sooner or later, three or more—super-Powers. Between these agglomerations lie large military in-between spaces, occasionally misdescribed as the Third World. Here world Powers and middle Powers manoeuvre with and against one another.

On the propagandist plane, it pays even the world Powers to leave at least one illusion to the international proletariat of small States: their feeling of importance in the United Nations and its Specialised Agencies. In any case, the treatment as sovereign and equal members given in these organisations to the serried ranks of small and minute States at least helps to boost their self-respect.

Within the frameworks of such quasi-orders, the laws of unorganised, partly-organised and confederate international societies fulfil functions of their own. It is their task to legitimise such quasi-orders in a manner comparable to the law of power within the State.

In fields of reciprocity which, from the point of view of power politics, are peripheral, international law is even permitted to fulfil other than purely ideological functions. The same is true of relations between Powers whose equality of strength neutralises the background threats of power politics.

This is even truer in exceptional situations as, for instance, when an international organisation for the care of earthquake victims is established. So long as a natural catastrophe takes place in time of peace and does not become an act of divine providence in time of war, the humanitarian altruism displayed in such contingencies is genuine enough. In such fleeting moments it is no illusion that an international law of co-ordination actually operates and fulfils its purported functions.

VI—DIAGNOSES, REMEDIES AND PROGNOSES

Attempts at making articulate medium- and long-range trends and evaluating critically diagnoses, remedies and prognoses of others are open to three serious objections: the difficulty, if not the impossibility, of making any value-judgments with more than a claim to relative objectivity; the need to answer questions in fields of which, the more remote they are from personal specialisation, any observer knows less than is desirable, and the inevitability of generalisations that are difficult to verify rationally.

To aim at perfectionism in these respects would be equivalent to renunciation altogether of such inter-disciplinary endeavours. It appears preferable to point out the risks of experiments of this type in a spirit of becoming self-criticism, but to undertake them in full awareness of these pitfalls.

Such investigations are needed for an additional reason. Any examination, however casual, of the literature of international law and relations yields an astounding harvest of subconscious or half-conscious value-judgments, made by academic writers. More or less charitably, these can be described as declarations of faith, ideologies or illusions. Yet they are hardly verifiable or better—with Karl Popper—falsifiable.

In this situation it appears to be the lesser evil neither to relapse into prescientific attitudes or unchecked value-judgements nor to take up a purely negative attitude of purist self-denial towards all value-judgments. There is an alternative that is probably preferable. It consists of undertaking such work in a manner that permits the reader the maximum of rational control and the opportunity to dissent, for reasons of his own, from any evaluation offered or to accept, with or without reservations, any diagnoses, remedies and prognoses suggested.

In this context, it becomes even worthwhile to examine critically past and present blueprints for international organisation the location of which may be considered to be left (or right) of reason (Lenin). The value of such schemes lies not so much in their positive contents as in the complementary analyses they suggest: Are such proposals utopias or ideologies in the technical meanings given to these terms by Karl Mannheim? In the former case, their realisation would presuppose a fundamental change, for instance, in contemporary world society. In the latter, such proposals are likely to serve on the international plane the purpose of hiding basic shortcomings of any existing *status quo* or of attempting to obtain tactical advantages in yet another exercise in one-upmanship.

The proposition that schemes for instant and complete disarmament or "world peace through world law," are utopian within the existing world systems does not imply any negative judgment. Within the French feudal system, the slogans of the bourgeois revolutionaries of the 18th century were utopian. Yet the social and political Revolution of 1789 made them realities. Conversely, the bourgeois counter-revolution against Jacobinism reduced the social-revolutionary utopias of freedom, equality and fraternity to ideological covers of the newly-created bourgeois society in France.

Finally, it is necessary to underline yet more strongly the difference between the ideas advanced in this Chapter and the so-called realistic treatment of international relations. It consists of the awareness which academic exercises in *Realpolitik* appear to lack that there is an ever-present possibility of transforming personal and group relations from society relations into community relations, and to reverse this process. What was and what is need not so remain.

It is possible to put a higher value on community relations than society relations as, for ultimately metaphysical reasons, the writer does. Anybody who shares this attitude will be inclined to speak of the danger of the degeneration of a community into a society and, in case of doubt, react positively to opportunities of transforming society relations into community relations.

If such an attitude is to be more than unworldly idealism, it is not enough to realise that one has the choice of basing any social relation on a society or community footing. It is important to know that this freedom of choice is greater in small than in big groups and easier to attain in personal than in impersonal relations.

The more firmly any particular social system is established the more difficult it is to change its fundamental character. In such cases, even the strongest players have but a limited and, from the higher to the lower ranks of this power hierarchy, decreasing freedom of choice.

Moreover, irrespective of the degreeof freedom of choice, the more fundamental and thorough a change is, the higher are its costs.

Decisive Realities

What, in a concrete historical situation, are realities, that is, circumstances that have to be taken into account—and even more so, what are decisive realities—depends on value-judgments on which wide disagreement is possible.

Perhaps the best attitude to value-judgments of others is to reflect on how often anybody who has to make judgments of his own has been wrong himself in his own past evaluations of situations and people. It is also rewarding to re-examine the writings of past decades from the point of view of how far the hypotheses, diagnoses and prognoses of distinguished authors of their times were confirmed or refuted by subsequent developments, and reflect on the difference, if any, which the implementation of their brain waves would have made.

In full awareness of these hard tests, a diagnosis of existing world society in fifteen guide-lines is offered:

(1) The doubling of world population within the next 25 years from three thousand million to six thousand million, especially in the world's poorest quarters, is likely.

(2) Continuation of the spoliation of the environment by *homo habilis,* who hardly deserves to be termed *homo sapiens,* is more probable than commensurate but expensive limitations of the present excessive exploitation of nature.

(3) In technologically developed countries with capitalist or State capitalist—frequently misdescribed as socialist or communist—forms of economic organisation, destructive tendencies towards ethical *laissez-faire* and nihilism are apparent. They favour anarchist threats to the State monopoly of legitimate force (Max Weber) and extreme—and probably more successful—authoritarian and totalitarian counter-reactions.

(4) This state has already been reached in most of the poor countries whose leading groups do not see any alternative but government by military juntas or one-party systems to maintain their privileged positions. The growing abyss between the standards of living of the technologically advanced nations and the proletariat of the poor countries, which, especially in the countryside, tend to develop backwards rather than forwards, accentuates these difficulties.

(5) The tendencies noted under (3) and (4) strengthen the general trend of a relapse of world civilisation into a mechanical and materialist type of neo-barbarism with atavistic tribal and racial ideologies.

(6) In States which owe their independence to the process of decolonisation, a neo-colonialism by detribalised urban politicians or leading tribes towards minorities is developing.

(7) The reintegration of the poor countries in the hierarchy of world society within the framework of the United Nations and other international institutions takes place in varying ways: competitive "development" or corruption aid, military alliances, treaties of friendship and association agreements with individual hegemonial Powers or behind the façades of sectional blocs.

(8) These blocs are organised around hegemonial Powers and serve to create political, economic or military macro-spaces.

(9) Contiguous macro-spaces are symptomatic for the present phase of an accelerating concentration of power in a few world Powers and a greater number of middle Powers. They are more significant than the counter-tendencies towards the atomisation and sublimation of the power of former overseas empires.

(10) The neutralism of small countries outside these blocs is little more than an ideology of middle and small States which find it increasingly difficult to convince themselves and others of the reality of their claims to leadership outside international organisations such as the United Nations and its Specialised Agencies.

(11) The state of armaments remains the most reliable barometer of international relations. Irrespective of whether absolute or relative standards are applied, the armaments of all States, and especially the super-Powers, have reached a cosmic scale. More convincingly than all protestations to the contrary, they demonstrate the strength of fear as the decisive motivation of international behaviour. This basic motivation has stamped international relations of the past and present as society relations which, essentially, are based on power.

(12) The existing world peace—in the sense of non-war—between the leading nations does not rest on the United Nations and its Specialised Agencies but on the background threat of nuclear co-extermination of the world Powers and the ruin of the rest of the world.

(13) The instability of this state of society peace which has already lasted longer than the whole inter-war period between the First and Second World Wars, is aggravated by three factors: the fallibility of little men in high positions in front of coloured telephones and nuclear push buttons, perhaps even under the influence of potent drugs;

the possibility of action based on false or falsely-interpreted information, and the growing danger that expanding nuclear conflicts will be triggered off by the increasing number of States with primitive nuclear equipment.

(14) Legal, moral and institutional superstructures of this world system of power politics in disguise offer opportunities for regular co-operation and manoeuvres by the Powers against one another on planes of sublimated power politics, with occasional excursions into genuine community politics, such as the United Nations Children's Fund.

(15) The analysis of multilateral treaties, "adopted" by international organisations—that is proposed for acceptance by them to their member States and others—provides reliable evidence of the significance of treaties such as the Genocide Convention or Human Rights Covenants of the United Nations. After the identification of the contracting parties, it still remains advisable to begin such investigations with a study of the reservations, contracting out provisions and exception clauses. Only then is it worthwhile analysing, if with becoming scepticism, the blaze of principles enunciated in the Preambles and chief articles of such humanitarian endeavours.

Ideologies, Utopias and Possibilities

What matters least in a sociological study of the successes and failures of a charitable organisation are the intentions of the operators. They can be taken for granted but, the Day of Judgment apart, are irrelevant. What matters is the help actually given, and the positive and negative effects of these efforts. The same applies to the ideologies and utopias of contemporary world society, offered in remarkable profusion.

Seven types of such efforts may be singled out from others:

(1) *Protection of Human Rights by International Law.* In international customary law, the legal personality of an entity depends on its recognition as a full or limited subject of international law by existing subjects of international law. In each case, the positive or negative answer to this question is not a dogmatic affirmation of faith but a question of evidence.

During the Second World War, it became evident that the Powers likely to be victorious were not prepared to subject themselves or, as after the First World War, some of their lesser allies to any international protection of minorities. Nor were the States subsequently created any more willing to accept comparable limitations of their newly acquired sovereignty.

Thus, the counsellors and spokesmen of minorities attempted to achieve the same end in more circuitous ways. If the protection of minorities was to be extended to all human beings, there would be no ethnic, linguistic, religious or other minority left that would not profit from such a generalisation of minorities protection. The international protection of human rights constituted a possible solution of an otherwise insoluble problem.

This argument was combined with a further thesis that was pressed for what it was worth and more: the individual as the direct bearer of rights and duties or, if not of rights, then at least of duties under international law. If accepted, this doctrine, which it would be hard to substantiate in international customary law, would have a desirable side effect. It would strengthen the claims for the automatic protection of human rights by international law beyond what was attained long ago by the protection of the minimum standards to be observed towards foreign nationals.

The heterogeneous character of the United Nations presents a major obstacle to the automatic protection of human rights by this world organisation. The United Nations must treat democratic States (in the Western sense), authoritarian States and totalitarian States on a footing of complete equality. Thus, it can hardly insist on maintaining that the denial of even the most primitive human rights by any member State to any of its subjects is incompatible with membership. This explains why, in the Charter of the United Nations, objectives such as the protection of human rights have been formulated so as not to create any legal obligations that are automatically binding on member States.

This dilemma became evident in the discussions and vote on the Declaration of Human Rights, adopted unanimously in 1948 by the General Assembly of the United Nations. So long as it was clear that the Declaration was not legally binding but was merely standard-setting and limited to moral goal-values, members vied with one another in the widest possible formulation of these moral rules. Yet, when the United Nations began to formulate legally binding covenants in these fields, this became a protracted business, and every member State took it for granted that it would not be bound automatically by any of these Covenants. Moreover, the human rights to be protected were subjected to a rapid process of shrinkage and far-reaching exception clauses, such as the legality of discrimination against non-nationals. Finally, potential contracting parties were granted the widest immunity from any verification by impartial organs of compliance with their obligations under the Human Rights Covenants.

In spite of all these concessions to national sovereignty, it has taken until 1976 for the two international Covenants on Human Rights of 1966 to obtain the required minimum of thirty-five ratifications and, thus, to enter into force between these Contracting Parties.

The typical behaviour of States on the universalist level of the United Nations in drafting conventions of this type is also demonstrated by the treatment of genocide in the post-1945 period. In the London War Crimes Charter of 1945, the punishment of crimes against humanity was limited to crimes which were connected with the preparation and conduct of the Second World War. In the Genocide Convention of 1948, genocide was limited to acts, committed with *intent* to achieve the destruction of national, ethnic, racial or religious groups. As an alternative to an international criminal tribunal, as yet not created, criminal proceedings against persons accused of such crimes are left to the courts of the country whose government or executive organs have ordered or carried out such mass murder. The chief effect of the Convention has been to make genocide a favoured invective for charging other States with unproven acts in a semi-legal terminology.

In the relations between States which have more ethical values in common than is the case on a global level, Conventions such as the European Convention on Human Rights of 1950 and its supplementary Protocols fulfil a more positive task. They contribute to the further integration of such sectional groupings and the creation of a common law, based on treaties and the practice of quasi-judicial and judicial organs.

(2) *Transnational Law.* Especially in the United States of America, the term *Transnational Law,* invented by Philip Jessup, has found a positive response. It is intended to describe legal relations which neither international nor national law is supposed to cover adequately.

In existing law, the purely negative character of this term limits its uses to systematic purposes. Even so, its existence encourages naturalist abuses: the deduction "from the nature of things" of legal rules which presuppose an inarticulate social environment of a community character and whose nourishing ground is usually one of the few systems of national law known to any particular transnational lawyer.

Related to these types of law-making under the counter are attempts to build a *Commercial Law of Nations* on general principles of law recognised by civilised nations. In such efforts, the operative incentive tends to be that of "finding" additional "transnational" legal rules for the protection of private property.

Actually, failures to achieve this object by way of multilateral conventions which proved unacceptable to capital-importing States might have suggested a different approach. It would probably have been academically less controversial and of greater assistance to private investors.

What is necessary is to face the unpalatable character of the prospects for private investments in poor countries. In contemporary world society, the export of private capital to countries other than the technologically most highly developed capitalist States or countries under their political or military control can be little more than lottery investments.

(3) *International Jus Cogens.* The international customary law of unorganised international society does not know of any *jus cogens.* The reason for this lies in the character of this type of international society. It lacks an order comparable to that of the State. Thus, there is little point in distinguishing between law that may be changed by agreement between the parties *(jus dispositivum)* and peremptory law that may not be so changed *(jus cogens).*

International systems of power politics have, at the most, quasi-orders of their own. This means a merely factual relation between the existence of such quasi-orders and the treaties strengthening and developing these systems. In case of doubt, the overthrow of any such political system also puts an end to the basic political treaties sustaining it.

On a consensual basis, subjects of international law may create as much *jus cogens* as they desire. Yet, such consensual *jus cogens* does not impose any legal obligations on third States. What is true is that the greater the number of parties to a treaty, the more difficult it is in fact to alter such consensual *jus cogens.* The seven Principles embodied in Article 2 of the Charter of the United Nations belong to this category.

The International Law Commission of the United Nations and the Vienna Diplomatic Conference of 1968—1969 incorporated the concept of international *jus cogens* in the 1969 Convention on the Law of Treaties. Yet neither the International Law Commission of the United Nations nor the Vienna Conference could agree on any binding list of rules of international customary law that were supposed to constitute *jus cogens.*

The fact that the concept of *jus cogens* has been embodied in the 1969 Convention is occasionally treated as a sufficient substitute for concrete evidence of the existence of *jus cogens* in international customary law. The further difficulty that the Convention is not yet in force—and, if and when in force, will be binding only on Contracting Parties—is pushed aside with an assertion of similar evidential cogency: that, at least on the issue of *jus cogens,* the Convention is but declaratory of existing international law.

What makes the terminology of *jus cogens* politically attractive are the opportunities it offers for purposes of ideological abuse. Thus, already before 1939, the term was employed with the object of discrediting the Peace Treaties of 1919—1920, and it is again available for similar purposes.

Jus cogens also offers a welcome device to escape from burdensome treaty obligations on the assertion of their incompatibility with an alleged rule of a peremptory character. Moreover, the "supreme international interest" in the form of an asserted rule of international *jus cogens* conveniently permits interference with treaty relations between third parties.

(4) *International Criminal Law.* International customary law knows as little of International Criminal Law as it does of rules of *jus cogens* which are comparable to those of a national *ordre public* or *public policy.* The reason is the same: in a world confederation, an overriding public order corresponding to those of national orders is lacking, as are international organs with automatic jurisdiction to apply and enforce such peremptory legal rules.

Apparent exceptions confirm the rule. The punishment of pirates and war criminals constitutes the exercise of an extraordinary national jurisdiction by States, in circumstances authorised by international customary law. A pirate ship which, at one time, may have been entitled to fly a national flag loses this privilege when she becomes a pirate ship. It may also be that such a ship was never under the jurisdiction of any subject of international law, Thus, in neither case, is there any State which is entitled to protest against the application of the national law of another State against the pirate ship or her crew.

Similarly, under international customary law, a belligerent or neutral Power may not claim that the rules of the Law of Armed Conflict which apply to prisoners of war are automatically extended to war criminals. These rules exist for the protection of prisoners who are entitled to carry arms and themselves observe the rules of the Law of Armed Conflict. The laws and customs of war contain but a single, and this merely an apparent, exception to this rule. In trials of alleged war criminals and spies, belligerents must observe minimum standards applicable in favour of any offender. For instance, the accused must have a fair trial and must not be subjected to any barbaric punishment.

Rules on the jurisdiction of national organs to apply internationally authorised—or, on a consensual basis, internationally prescribed—national criminal law are international criminal law in a but limited meaning of the term. The same applies to mutual assistance given to each other by State organs in proceedings leading to the extradition of accused or convicted persons.

On the confederate level, more far-reaching attempts to create international criminal organs have remained in the limbo of draft conventions. Even so, like other proposals for reform which go beyond whatever happens to be the degree of international integration feasible at any time on a global scale, such drafts have a symptomatic relevance. They stimulate reflection on the reasons why, at this particular phase of the evolution of world society, they are condemned to the shadowy existence of ideologies or utopias.

(5) *International Parliamentary Diplomacy.* Several features of contemporary international institutions prompt sanguine conclusions on the character and functions of these consensual superstructures. Among them may be enumerated the multitude of international institutions with organs in which all member States are represented; the wide scope of their jurisdiction; the length of their public sessions; debates on procedure and other comparable exercises; the inundation of delegations with relevant and irrelevant material; the self-propagation of committees and sub-committees; the ministrations of international and national civil servants to the members of delegations and the contact with accredited correspondents of the world press and other mass media. The plethora of these activities, coupled with the needs of all concerned to convince themselves and others of their own relevance, can easily create the impression of a new phenomenon in the making: democratic and quasi-parliamentary forms of international diplomacy.

If, in addition, in exceptional cases such as that of the General Conference of the International Labour Organisation, at least half of the national delegations are nominated by their governments on the recommendation of the sectional interests concerned and, in voting, national delegates are free from government instructions, the illusion of international democracy in action is further strengthened. For reasons of formal universality and international *camaraderie,* it is also charitably overlooked that, in the United Nations and its Specialised Agencies, the majority of the delegates who are supposed to practise international parliamentary democracy represent authoritarian or totalitarian régimes.

Moreover, it appears far-fetched to apply the analogy of parliamentary representation to organs which, on almost all matters of substance, are limited to advisory functions but lack decision-making powers.

As with other ideologies and utopias discussed and to be discussed, this terminology has its dangers. It contributes to the mollification of a typical system of power politics in disguise and diverts attention from the constitutional weaknesses of its confederate superstructures.

(6) *International Functionalism.* As far back as the second half of the nineteenth century, the founders of the International and, subse-

quently, Universal Postal Union had a splendid idea. They realised that if the whole world could be organised as a uniform postal territory, this would assure the best postal services.

To everybody's benefit, this was done. Why should this experiment not be extended to other fields? There are many tasks which can be performed better in co-operation, with the aid of functional institutions, than in isolation and competition. In this way, it might even be possible to achieve indirectly another object: to outflank power politics. Before the guardians of national sovereignty became aware of it, a system of open power politics or politics in disguise might be irrevocably transformed into a functional world community.

At first sight, the creation of the Specialised Agencies of the United Nations may be viewed as a series of such attempts. They extend from areas covering the protection of labour and exchange parities via education and liberalisation of trade to development aid, the freedom of the seas and the international control of nuclear energy.

Functionalists tend to overlook but one small point. Irrespective of what the rest of the world wants—and it is improbable that most of the old, as well as new, middle Powers and small States want anything different—the governments and bureaucracies of the world Powers are little inclined to share their governmental and administrative monopolies with other government representatives and competing sets of international bureaucrats. They are, however, willing to create confederate international organisations with essentially consultative and prelegislative functions and, within a margin of tolerance, let them behave as if they were the organs of a functional international community.

The foundation of the German Customs Union *(Zòllverein)* of 1833 and the three European Communities of 1951 and 1957 furnish reversals of this situation and, as regional or sectional exceptions, confirm the general rule. For the forces which, in the nineteenth century, aimed at German unification, the German Customs Union was but an economic means to a political end. Similarly, the fathers of the European Communities knew that, in the period immediately following the Second World War, any direct political union of Western Europe was psychologically unacceptable to the victims and enemies of Nazism, if not Germany. They wanted this unification but were astute enough to seek this objective through the back door of international functionalism.

Wherever and to the extent to which the common will to attain such unity exists, functionalism is a realistic means of avoiding a waste of energy by competition between units which are no longer viable as independent entities or less powerful than they would be if they pooled their resources.

It is an open question whether this supranational *élan* in Western Europe has evaporated. Thus, only the future can tell whether these Communities amount merely to a West European Confederation, *l'Europe des patries,* or whether the infusion of new blood into the Communities will lead to a new advance in functional federalism.

Even if this common will proved stronger than at present is apparent and lead to a federation of Western Europe, this would mean merely the creation of a new if artificial great Power in a world society that remains in character unchanged. It would hardly constitute a staging-post on the road to supranational functionalism on a world scale.

(7) *Reform of the United Nations.* There is an ambiguous way of formulating proposals for the mitigation or elimination of the shortcomings of the existing system of world power politics in disguise. It is to present such suggestions under the rubric of a reform of the United Nations.

In form, such proposals may appear to involve no more than changes in the voting patterns of organs of the United Nations. Suggestions for limiting or abolishing the right of veto of the permanent members of the Security Council belong to this category. Actually, any such change would make possible majority decisions against one or more of the world Powers and thus alter fundamentally the character of the United Nations as an essentially hegemonial world confederation.

This would apply even more to proposals of a similar hue regarding the pacific settlement of legal and political disputes and the peaceful change of any existing *status quo.* Formally, it would suffice to transform the non-binding or optional character of available procedures into a binding and obligatory jurisdiction of the relevant political and legal organs of the United Nations.

The same is true of a whole series of other proposals: the creation of economic organs with automatic power of decision regarding all members of the United Nations, and not only those who submit themselves voluntarily to the jurisdiction of institutions such as the Bretton Woods Organisations or the General Agreement on Tariffs and Trade; the establishment of *ad hoc* or permanent international police forces with delegated powers to act, or the abolition of national armaments by majority decisions.

Regarding such projects, two alternatives exist: either they mean but an apparent development of existing confederate organisations or organs which, as does the United Nations Conference on Trade and Development, make less impact than noise, or they constitute embryonic and surreptitious developments of a federal character.

Whether any such proposals can be realised in any particular historical situation or whether they are merely tactical moves in games of one-upmanship is easy to find out.

Two tests will assist in this task:

(1) Is it likely that, as would be required under the Charter of the United Nations, any of these blueprints are acceptable to two-thirds of the members of the General Assembly?

(2) Is it likely that any such changes in the Charter would be ratified by two-thirds of the members of the United Nations, including all permanent members of the Security Council?[3]

Observers and Actors

For a considerable period, our world has been dragged along by a quaint seven-tiger team: population explosion; spoliation of the human environment; growing inflation; increasing financial inequality between rich and poor countires; racial discrimination; cosmic armaments, and an inherently unstable nuclear equilibrium.

In a situation fraught with chronic dangers of this magnitude, observers of international relations and actors on the international scene fulfil different functions. In such an atmosphere of glaring contradictions between appearances and realities, observers alone can afford the luxury of calling a spade a spade. To indulge in euphemisms would not alter these realities. It would merely demean academic analysis to another propaganda service in aid of covering up these grim realities.

Actually, detached analyses may help the player to avoid anything that may contribute to the actual deterioration of the existing situation. Should any actor be able to do anything that actually improved this situation, he would deserve a Nobel Prize. If he and other statesmen succeeded in transforming the existing world society into a world community, those engaged in this truly noble task would deserve a super-Nobel Prize.

In any case, one thing only should be impossible for a generation which has survived two World Wars and, in one form or another, has already heard in previous pre-war, war and post-war periods all the slogans and patent solutions offered again as novelties in our time. It is to fall again for the siren songs of power politics in disguise and crown its bards in anticipation of deeds yet to be preformed.

Is it not more appropriate to follow the example of doubting Thomas and believe only what one clearly sees? Even so, it is advisable first to ascertain whether what one sees or imagines one sees is more than a *fata morgana.*

[3] Readers interested in the writer's relativist approach to problems of international planning and legislation may wish to consult Part Three of *Power Politics. A Study of World Society* (3rd ed., 1964), p. 519 *et seq.*, or *Manual of International Law* (6th ed., 1976), Chapter 12.

SUGGESTIONS FOR INTER-DISCIPLINARY READING

I—Attempt at an Empirical Synthesis

Augustinus: *De Civitate Dei* (c. 413-426)
Campanella, T.: *Civitas Solis* (1620)
Curtis, L.: *Civitas Dei* (1934)
Huber, M.: *Gesellschaft und Humanitaet* (1948)
Jenks, C. W.: *The Will of the World Community as the Basis of Obligation in International Law* in *Law, Freedom and Welfare* (1963)
Lauterpacht, H.: *The Nature of International Law and General Jurisprudence* (12 *Economica* 1932)
Lippman, W.: *The Good Society* (1937)
Verdross, A.: *Statisches und dynamisches Naturrecht* (1971)
Wallas, G.: *The Great Society* (1914)
Wolff, Chr. von: *Jus Gentium Methodo Scientifica Pertractatum* (1749)

II—Society and Community Models

Andresky, S.: *Social Sciences as Sorcery* (1972)
Burton, J. W.: *Systems, States, Diplomacy and Rules* (1968)
Carter, F. W.: *Dubrovnik (Ragusa). A Classical City State* (1972)
Collingwood, R. G.: *The New Leviathan* (1942)
Collins, L. (ed.): *The Uses of Models in the Social Sciences* (1974)
Cobb, R. W., and Elder, C.: *International Community* (1972)
Cooley, Ch. H.: *Human Nature and the Social Order* (1902)
Deutsch, K. W.: *The Nerves of Government* (1966)
Durkheim, E.: *De la division du travail social* (1893)
Easton, D.: *A Framework for Social Analysis* (1965)
Gluckman, M.: *Politics, Law and Ritual in Tribal Society* (1971)
Green, L. C.: *Law and Society* (1975)
Jacoby, E. G.: *Die moderne Gesellschaft im sozialwissenschaftlichen Denken von Ferdinand Toennies* (1971)
Kropotkin, Prince Peter: *Mutual Aid* (1904)
Lévy-Strauss, C.: *La Pensée Sauvage* (1968)
Lorenz, K.: *On Aggression* (1966)
Macmurray, J.: *Creative Society* (1938)
Maine, Sir Henry Sumner: *Ancient Law* (1861)
Marx, K.: *Zur Judenfrage (Deutsch-Franzoesische Jahrbuecher 1843/44)*
Merton, R. K.: *Social Theory and Social Structure* (1968)
Montagu, A. (ed.): *Man and Aggression* (1973)
Niebuhr, R.: *Moral Man and Immoral Society* (1934)
Northrop, F. S.C.: *Philosophical Anthropology and Practical Politics* (1960)
Olsen, M. E. (ed.): *Power in Societies* (1970)
Parsons, T.: *Societies: Evolutionary and Comparative Perspectives* (1966)

Popper, K.: *The Open Society and its Enemies* (1950)
Scherer, J.: *Contemporary Community* (1972)
Schwarzenberger, G.: *The Frontiers of International Law* (1962—Chap. 1: The Three Types of Law)
Sperlich, P. W.: *Conflict and Harmony in Human Affairs* (1971)
Spinoza, B. de: *Tractatus Theologico-Politicus* (1670)
Toennies, F.: *Gemeinschaft und Gesellschaft* (1887)
Toynbee, A.: *A Study of History,* Vol. 12: *Reconsiderations* (1961)
Weber, M.: *Wirtschaft und Gesellschaft* (1922)
Zimmern, A.: *The Greek Commonwealth* (1915)
Zweig, F.: *The Quest for Fellowship* (1965)

III—World Community?

Aron, R.: *Paix et guerre entre les nations* (1962)
Barston, R. P.: *The Other Powers* (1973)
Bell, C.: *The Conventions of Crisis* (1971)
Brandon, H.: *The Retreat of American Power* (1973)
Brow, N.: *European Security 1972-1980* (1972)
Buchan, A.: *An Expedition to the Poles* (29 *Year Book of World Affairs*—1975); *Power and Equilibrium in the 1970's* (1973)
Bull, H.: *The Control of the Arms Race* (1965)
Burton, J. W.: *World Society* (1972)
Butterfield, H., and Wight, M. (eds.): *Diplomatic Investigations* (1966)
Carr, E. H.: *The Twenty Years Crisis 1919-1939* (1939)
Claude, I. L.: *Power and International Relations* (1962)
Cox, R. W., and Jacobsen, H.: *The Anatomy of Influence* (1973)
Frankel, J.: *International Politics* (1973)
Harrod, J.: *Trade Union Foreign Policy* (1972)
Hexter, J. H.: *The History Primer* (1972)
Hinsley, F. H.: *Nationalism and the International System* (1973)
James, A.: *The Politics of Peace-Keeping* (1969)
Jouvenel, B. de: *Du Pouvoir* (1945); *De la Souveraineté* (1955)
Joynt, C.: *The Analysis of Crises* (28 *Year Book of World Affairs* 1974)
Kaufmann, G.: *Il Systema Globale* (1974)
Kissinger, H.: *The World Restored. Metternich, Castlereagh and the Problem of Peace 1812-1822* (1957)
Knorr, K.: *Power and Wealth. The Political Economy of International Power* (1973)
Kyellen, R.: *Die Grossmaechte der Gegenwart* (1914)
Lasswell, H. D.: *World Politics and Personal Insecurity* (1935)
Manning, C. A.: *The Nature of International Society* (1962)
Martin, L. W.: *The Sea in Modern Strategy* (1967)
Modelski, G.: *Principles of World Politics* (1972)
Morgan, R. (ed.): *The Study of International Affairs* (1972)
Morgenthau, H.-J.: *Politics in the 20th Century* (3 vols.—1962)
Owen, D.: *The Politics of Defence* (1972)
Pierre, A. J.: *Nuclear Politics* (1972)
Porter, B. (ed.): *The Aberystwyth Papers: International Politics 1919-1969* (1972)
Rosenau, J. N., and Others (eds.): *The Analysis of International Politics* (1972)
Russett, B. M. (ed.): *Peace, War and Numbers* (1972)
Ruyssen, Th.: *La Société Internationale* (1950)

Schwarzenberger, G.: *Power Politics. A Study of World Society* (1941—3rd ed. 1964); *Ueber die Machtpolitik hinaus?* (1968)
Singer, H. R.: *Weak States in a World of Powers* (1972)
Spanier, J. W.: *Games Nations Play* (1972)
Sperlich, P. W.: *Conflict and Harmony in Human Affairs* (1971)
Tanter, R., and Ullmann, R. H. (eds.): *Theory and Policy in International Relations* (1972)
Thucydides (translated by Thomas Hobbes): *The Peloponnesian War* (1676) or *History of the Peloponnesian War* (translated by R. Warner—1972)
Ulam, A.: *The Rivals: America and Russia since World War II* (1973)
Vasquez, M. S.: *Zones of Influence* (27 *Year Book of World Affairs*—1973)
Wheeler-Bennett, J., and Nicholls, A.: *The Semblance of Peace* (1972)
Whitaker, B. Ch.: *The Fourth World* (1972)

IV—World law?

Barkun, M.: *Law without Sanctions* (1968)
Brierly, J. L. (ed. Sir Humphrey Waldock): *The Law of Nations* (1963)
Cheng, Bin: *The General Principles of Law as Applied by International Courts and Tribunals* (1953)
Corbett, P. E.: *From International to World Law* (1969)
Delos, J. T.: *La Société Internationale et les Principes du Droit Public* (1950)
Deutsch, K., and Hoffmann, S. (eds.): *The Relevance of International Law* (1968)
Falk, R. A.: *The Status of Law in International Society* (1970)
Fawcett, J. E. S.: *The Law of Nations* (1968)
Guggenheim, P.: *Traité de Droit international public* (2 vols.—1953)
Henkin, L.: *How Nations Behave* (1968)
Jenks, C. W.: *A New World Law?* (1969)
Lauterpacht, H.: *The Function of Law in the International Community* (1933)
Niemeyer, G.: *Law without Force* (1941)
O'Connell, D. P.: *International Law* (2 vols.—1970)
Okeke, Ch. N.: *Controversial Subjects of Contemporary International Law* (1974)
Rousseau, Ch.: *Principes de droit international public (Recueil,* Hague Academy of International Law, Vol. 93—1958)
Schwarzenberger, G.: *The Fundamental Principles of International Law (Recueil,* Hague Academy of International Law, Vol. 87—1955)
Simma, B.: *Das Reziprozitaetselement in der Entstehung des voelkerrechtlichen Gewohnheitsrechts* (1970); *Das Reziprozitaetselement im Zustandekommen voelkerrechtlicher Vertraege* (1972)
Tunkin, G.: *Voelkerrechtstheorie* (1972)
Verdross, A.: *Die Einheit des rechtlichen Weltbildes auf Grundlage der Voelkerrechtsverfassung* (1923)
—, and Others: *Voelkerrecht* (1964)
Visscher, Ch. de: *Théories et Réalités en Droit International Public* (1960)

V—World Order?

Alexandrowicz, Ch. H.: *The Law of Global Communications* (1971)
Aron, R.: *République impériale. Les Etas-Unis dans le monde 1945-1972* (1973)

Bocard, L.: *Le Massacre des Indiens* (1969)
Bowett, D. W.: *The Law of International Institutions* (1975)
Brown, E. D.: *The Legal Regime of Hydrospace* (1971)
Falk, A.R., and Mendlovisz, S.H.: *The Strategy of World Order* (5 vols.—1966—)
Feller, A. H.: *United Nations and World Community* (1952)
Friedmann, W.: *The Changing Structure of International Law* (1964)
Goodrich, L. M., Hambro, E., and Simons, A. P.: *The Charter of the United Nations* (1969)
Gutteridge, J. A. C.: *The United Nations in a Changing World* (1970)
Haas, E. B., and Others: *Conflict Management by International Organisations* (1972)
Haas, M.: *International Conflict* (1974)
Herz, J. H.: *International Politics in the Atomic Age* (1960)
Heydte, F. A. Freiherr von der: *Die Geburtsstunde des souveraenen Staates* (1952)
Higgins,R.: *The Development of International Law through the Political Organs of the United Nations* (1963)
Holbraad, C. (ed.): *Super Powers and World Order* (1971)
Kahn, H.: *On Escalation* (1965)
Kelsen, H.: *The Law of the United Nations* (1950-51)
Kohn, H.: *World Order in Historical Perspective* (1942)
McDougal, M. S., and Associates: *Studies in World Public Order* (1960)
—, and Feliciano, F. P.: *Law and Minimum World Public Order* (1961)
Moore, J. N.: *Law and the Indo-China War* (1972)
Schiffer, W.: *The Legal Community of Mankind* (1954)
Schwarzenberger, G.: *The League of Nations and World Order* (1936); *International Law and Order* (1971)
Stone, J.: *Aggression and World Order* (1958)
Touscoz, J.: *Le principe d'effectivité dans l'ordre international* (1964)
Tunkin, G.: *Der ideologische Kampf und das Voelkerrecht* in E. Menzel (ed.): *Drei sowjetische Beitraege zur Voelkerrechtslehre* (1969)
Zimmern, A.: *The League of Nations and the Rule of Law* (1936)

VI—Diagnoses, Remedies and Prognoses

Beer, S.: *Platform for Change* (1975)
Black, C. E., and Falk, R. A. (eds.): *The Future of the International Legal Order* (4 vols.—1969-72)
Brierly, J. L.: *The Outlook for International Law* (1944)
Carr, E. H.: *Conditions of Peace* (1942)
Clarke, G., and Sohn, L. B.: *World Peace through World Law* (1966)
Fawcett, J. E. S.: *The Application of the European Convention on Human Rights* (1969)
Flechtheim, O. R.: *History and Futurology* (1966)
Frankel, J.: *Contemporary International Theory and the Behaviour of States* (1973)
Friedmann, W., and Others (eds.): *Transnational Law in a Changing Society* (1972)
Fromm, E.: *The Sane Society* (1956)
Groom, A. J. R., and Taylor, P. (eds.): *Functionalism* (1975)

Hahlo, H. R., and Others (eds.): *Nationalism and the Multinational Enterprise* (1973)
Hamilton, A., Madison, J., and Jay, J.: *The Federalist* (1787-88)
Horkheimer, M.: *Eclipse of Reason* (1947)
James, A. (ed.): *Bases of International Order* (1973)
Jenks, C. W.: *The Common Law of Mankind* (1958)
Jessup, Ph. C.: *Transnational Law*; (1956) *Parliamentary Diplomacy (Recueil,* Hague Academy of International Law, Vol. 89—1956); *The Present State of Transnational Law* in M. Bos (ed.): *The Present State of International Law and Other Essays* (1973)
Kahn, H., and Bruce-Briggs, B.: *Things to Come* (1972)
Kalmus, H.: *Living Together Without Man* (25 *Year Book of World Affairs*—1971)
Laski, H.: *Reflections on the Revolution of Our Time* (1943)
Lauterpacht, H.: *An International Bill of the Rights of Man* (1945); *International Law and Human Rights* (1950)
Le Bon, G.: *The World in Revolt* (1921)
Lieber, R. J.: *Theory and World Politics* (1973)
McNair, Lord: *The General Principles of Law Recognised by Civilised Nations* (33 *British Year Book of International Law*—1957); *Hersch Lauterpacht* (10 *International and Comparative Law Quarterly*—1961)
Mann, A. F.: *Reflections on a Commercial Law of Nations* (33 *British Year Book of International Law*—1957)
Mannheim, K.: *Ideology and Utopia* (1936); *Diagnosis of our Time* (1943)
Mitrany, D.: *A Working Peace System* (1966)
Nostradamus, M.: *Les Prophéties* (1568)
Owen, H. (ed.): *The Next Phase in Foreign Policy* (1973)
Pentland, C. C.: *Neofunctionalism* (27 *Year Book of World Affairs*—1973)
Picht, G.: *Mut zur Utopie* (1969)
Plischke, E. (ed.): *Systems of Integrating the International Community* (1964)
Roeling, B. V. A.: *International Law in an Expanded World* (1960)
Russell, B.: *Has Man a Future?* (1961)
Schlochauer, H.-J.: *Die Idee des ewigen Friedens* (1953)
Schmitt, C.: *Der Nomos der Erde* (1950)
Schwarzenberger, G.: *Foreign Investments and International Law* (1969—Chap. 12)
Sewell, J. P.: *Functionalism and World Politics* (1966)
Sorokin, P. A.: *Russia and the United States* (1950)
Vallat, Sir Francis (ed.): *Human Rights* (1972)
Vincent, R. J.: *The Functions of Functionalism in International Relations* (27 *Year Book of World Affairs*—1973)
Waltz, K. N.: *Man, the State and War* (1959)

INDEX